# My Bangladeshi Cookbook

A Cookbook with 130+Desi Recipes

**Vikas Jaffrey**

Copyright © 2023 by Vikas Jaffrey

**All rights reserved worldwide.**

Without the publisher's express consent, no portion of this book may be duplicated or communicated in any way, whether it be electronically or mechanically, including by photocopying, recording, or information storing and retrieval systems.

**Warning-Disclaimer**

This Bangladeshi Cookbook aims to give people ideas about Bangladeshi recipes. We can not guarantee that everyone will be successful by following the book.

# CONTENTS

**BANGLADESHI CUISINE** — 9

**LIST OF BANGLADESHI DISHES** — 11

**MOST POPULAR FOOD** — 16

**BREAKFAST RECIPES** — 18
- Balushahi Recipe — 18
- Salted Rough Crackers — 19
- Nolen Gurer Cake — 20
- Teller Poa Pitha Recipe — 21
- Mini Moglai Porota Recipe — 22
- Dal Puri Recipe — 23
- Pizza Recipe Without Oven — 24
- Dough Paratha Recipe — 25
- Fried Lentil Patties Recipe — 26
- Maltova Cake Recipe — 27
- Easy Cupcake Recipe — 28
- Chira Chop Recipe — 29
- Pav Bread Recipe — 30
- Milk Chocolate Cake Recipe — 31
- Fulko Luchi Recipe — 32
- Handi Kebab — 33
- Egg Pizza Sandwich Recipe — 34
- Stick Kebab Recipe — 35
- Eggplant Fritters Recipe — 36
- Crispy Egg Ball Recipe — 37
- Semolina Sujir Biscuit Pitha Recipe — 38
- Crispy Piyaju Recipe — 38
- Sauteed Butter Garlic Mushrooms Recipe — 39
- Vanilla Cup Of Cake Recipe — 40
- Chickpea Recipe — 41
- Crispy Vaja Puli Pitha Recipe — 42
- Butter Cookie Recipe — 43
- Narkel Naru Recipe — 44
- Egg Sandwich — 44
- Potato Cheese Balls — 45
- Egg Salad Recipe — 46

**RICE RECIPES** — 47
- Sweet Rice Recipe — 47
- Vuna Khichuri Recipe — 48
- Chinese Fried Rice Recipe With Shrimp — 49
- Non-Sticky Pulao Recipe — 50
- Spicy Fried Puffed Rice — 51

**MEAT RECIPES** — 52
- Beef Curry With Potatoes — 52
- Bangladeshi Beef Chili Recipe — 54
- Duck Curry With Coconut Milk — 55
- Chicken With Cauliflower — 56
- Homemade Chicken Bun Recipe — 57
- Yogurt And Cilantro Marinated Grilled Chicken — 58
- Spicy Chicken Spaghetti Recipe — 59
- Chicken Roast Recipe — 60
- Chicken Curry Recipe — 61
- Homestyle Chicken Korma — 62
- Easy Beef Tahari Recipe — 63
- Mutton Curry With Potatoes — 64
- Cattle Head Vuna — 65
- Stir-Fried Beef — 66
- Beef Cabernet — 66
- Beef Brain Bhuna — 67
- Chicken Noodle Soup Recipe — 68
- Chicken Steak Recipe Without Oven — 69
- Chicken Chow Mein — 69

**BEVERAGE RECIPES** — 71
- Pineapple Juice Recipe — 71
- Green Mango Juice — 71
- Milk Tea Recipe — 72
- Special Sharbat Recipe — 72
- Sweet, Sour, Spicy Tea — 73
- Sweet, Sour Tamarind Juice — 73
- Fish Curry With Bean — 74

**FISH RECIPES** — 75
- Fish Head With Mung Dal Recipe — 75
- Rui Macher Jhaal Kalia – Spicy Fish Kalia — 76

| | |
|---|---|
| Bhapa Chingri –Steamed Shrimp With Mustard | 77 |
| Hilsa Fish Fry | 78 |
| Mashed Tilapia Fish | 78 |
| Hilsa Fish In Mustard Sauce | 79 |
| Rohu Fish Kaliya | 80 |
| Spinach With Shrimp | 81 |
| Okra With Shrimp Recipe | 81 |
| Steamed Hilsa Fish Recipe | 82 |
| Rohu Fish Vuna Recipe | 82 |
| Parshe Fish Recipe | 83 |
| Easy Hate Makha Ilish Recipe | 84 |
| Bottle Gourd Recipe With Shrimp | 84 |
| Hilsa Fish With Banana | 85 |
| Delicious Fish Kebab Recipe | 85 |
| Hilsa With Spinach | 86 |
| Eggplant With Prawn Recipe | 87 |
| Hilsa Pilaf Rice Recipe | 87 |
| Bangladeshi Small Fish Recipe | 88 |
| Hilsa Fish With Arum | 89 |
| Rohu Fish With Eggplant | 90 |
| Homemade Fish Finger Recipe | 90 |
| Spicy Fish Fry | 91 |
| Mawa Ghat Ilish Lej Vorta | 92 |

**VEGETABLE RECIPES** 93

| | |
|---|---|
| Vegetable Egg Noodles Recipe | 93 |
| Stir-Fried Cabbage With Garlic And Bengali Spices | 94 |
| Dharosh Bhaji (Okra) | 95 |
| Palong Shaak Bhaji – Spinach Bhaji | 95 |
| Chichinga Bhaji – Fried Zuchhini | 96 |
| Vegetable Pulao | 97 |
| Begun Bhaji (Fried Eggplant) | 97 |
| Lau Bhaji – Bottlegourd Bhaji | 98 |
| Special Mix Veg Recipe | 99 |
| Chicken Curry With Potato | 100 |
| Potato Stuffed Paratha Recipe | 101 |
| Potato Chop Recipe | 102 |
| Potato Pakora Recipe | 103 |
| Long Bean Recipe | 104 |
| Chinese Vegetable Recipe | 105 |
| Papaya With Mung Dal | 106 |
| Potato Curry Recipe | 107 |

**DESSERT RECIPES** 108

| | |
|---|---|
| Milk And Egg Caramel Pudding Recipe | 108 |
| Roshogolla Recipe | 109 |
| Easy Sujir Barfi Halwa Recipe | 110 |
| Mashed Green Mango | 111 |
| Mango Chutney | 111 |
| Gulab Jamun Recipe | 112 |
| Plum Chutney | 113 |
| Vermicelli In Milk Recipe | 113 |
| Egg Halwa Recipe | 114 |
| Milk Cookies Recipe | 115 |
| Chanar Jilapi Recipe | 116 |
| Malai Cake Recipe | 117 |
| Falooda Recipe | 118 |
| Instant Shahi Tukra Recipe | 119 |
| Spicy Kashmiri Achar Recipe | 119 |
| Sweet Yogurt Recipe | 120 |
| Sago Kesari Recipe | 121 |
| Powder Roshmalai | 122 |

**Exceptional Recipe** 123

| | |
|---|---|
| Egg Biryani Recipe | 123 |
| Ilish Pulao Recipe | 124 |
| Banana Cake Recipe | 125 |
| Palm Cake | 126 |
| Instant Mango Pickle Recipe | 127 |
| Jackfruit With Prawn Recipe | 128 |
| Drumstick Curry Recipe | 129 |
| Banana Chips Recipe | 130 |
| Rice Flour Vape/Bhapa Pitha Recipe | 130 |
| Chitoi Pitha Recipe Without Rice Flour | 131 |
| Chotpoti Recipe With Special Spices Mix | 132 |
| Green Banana Cutlet | 134 |
| Elephant Arum Stem Recipe | 135 |
| Brinjal/Eggplant/Aubergine Paste | 136 |
| Mashed Cilantro/Coriander Leaves | 136 |
| Rice Pudding With Jaggery | 137 |
| Naan | 138 |

**CONCLUSION** 139

# INTRODUCTION

Bangladesh, officially known as the People's Republic of Bangladesh, is in South Asia. It communicates its borders with India to the west, north, and east and Myanmar (Burma) to the southeast. With a population exceeding 170 million, Bangladesh is one of the most densely colonized countries in the world. The capital and biggest city of Bangladesh is Dhaka.

Bangladesh has a rich history that dates back thousands of years. It was part of various empires and dynasties, including the Maurya Empire, Gupta Empire, Pala Empire, and the Bengal Sultanate. European traders arrived in the region in the 15th century, and it eventually came under British rule as part of British India. After a long struggle, Bangladesh emerged as an independent nation in 1971 following a war of liberation from Pakistan.

Geographically, Bangladesh is a land of rivers, with the mighty Ganges (known as the Padma) and Brahmaputra rivers converging in its fertile plains, forming the largest delta in the world. The country also dwells on the Sundarbans, the world's most extensive mangrove forest, and a UNESCO World Heritage Site, which provides a unique habitat for diverse wildlife, including the Royal Bengal Tiger.

The economy of Bangladesh has experienced significant growth over the past few decades. It is primarily an agrarian economy, with agriculture employing a large portion of the population. The country produces rice, jute, tea, and various fruits and vegetables. Additionally, the ready-made garment industry has played a crucial role in boosting the country's economy and significantly contributing to its export earnings.

Despite its economic progress, Bangladesh faces various challenges. Poverty, overpopulation, and inadequate infrastructure remain significant concerns. Besides, the country is prone to natural disasters such as cyclones, floods, and droughts, often devastatingly affecting its population and economy. However, in recent years, Bangladesh has made significant strides in poverty reduction, improving healthcare, and expanding access to education.

Culturally, Bangladesh is a vibrant nation with a diverse mix of traditions and customs. Bengali is the official language, and Islam is the predominant religion, with Muslims constituting most of the population. Bengali literature, music, and arts have a rich heritage and have produced renowned figures such as Nobel Laureate Rabindranath Tagore.

Bangladesh is also known for its warm hospitality and delicious cuisine. Bengali cuisine is famous for its spices and flavors, with popular dishes including rice, fish curry, lentils, and various vegetable preparations. The country's traditional attire for women is the sari, while men commonly wear the lungi or panjabi.

Bangladesh has progressed in various sectors in recent years, including education, healthcare, and women's empowerment. The country has achieved remarkable gender parity in primary and secondary education and has made significant strides in reducing maternal and child mortality rates.

Bangladesh is a parliamentary democracy with a President as the head of circumstances and a Prime Minister as the head of government. The political landscape has been dominated by two major political parties, the Awami League and the Bangladesh Nationalist Party (BNP). However, there are several other political parties as well, contributing to a multi-party system.

The country has made notable progress in achieving social development goals. Bangladesh has significantly reduced poverty levels over the past few decades. According to the World Bank, the deprivation rate dropped from over 40% in the early 1990s to around 20% in recent years. This achievement is attributed to various factors, including increased agricultural productivity, the growth of the garment industry, and the expansion of microfinance initiatives.

Bangladesh has also made significant progress in improving healthcare outcomes. The country has successfully reduced child mortality rates and improved access to healthcare services. The introduction of community health workers, known as "Shasthya Kormis," has played a crucial role in providing primary healthcare services to rural areas.

Education is another area where Bangladesh has made substantial strides. The country has made marked progress in achieving universal primary education and improving literacy rates. The government has implemented initiatives to increase school enrollment, enhance the quality of education, and provide scholarships to marginalized students.

One of the notable achievements of Bangladesh is its success in the field of microfinance. The Grameen Bank, founded by Nobel Laureate Muhammad Yunus, pioneered the concept of microcredit, providing small loans to impoverished individuals, particularly women, to start their businesses. This initiative has empowered millions of Bangladeshis, alleviating poverty and fostering entrepreneurship.

Bangladesh is also known for its vibrant cultural heritage. The country has an affluent tradition of music, dance, and literature. Traditional folk music, known as "Baul," is popular, along with classical music forms like "Rabindra Sangeet," which celebrates the works of Rabindranath Tagore. The annual "Ekushey Book Fair" in Dhaka is a significant event for book lovers, showcasing a wide range of literature.

In recent years, Bangladesh has also made efforts to promote tourism. The country offers diverse tourist attractions, including historical sites like the ancient city of Bagerhat, archaeological sites of Mahasthangarh and Paharpur, and natural wonders like Cox's Bazar, the longest sea beach in the world. The government has taken steps to improve infrastructure and hospitality services and promote eco-tourism to attract international visitors.

Furthermore, Bangladesh has been actively engaged in addressing environmental challenges. As a low-lying deltaic country, it is highly vulnerable to the outcomes of climate change, including growing sea levels, increased frequency of cyclones, and erratic weather patterns. The government has undertaken initiatives to promote sustainable development, renewable energy, and climate adaptation measures to mitigate these challenges.

Bangladesh has also contributed to United Nations peacekeeping missions, providing troops and personnel to various countries. The country's armed forces have gained recognition for their contributions to international peacekeeping efforts.

Overall, Bangladesh is a nation that has made remarkable progress in various spheres, including economic development, social welfare, and cultural preservation. Despite challenges, the country strives for inclusive growth and sustainable development, aiming to enhance the lives of its people and donate to regional and global cooperation.

## BANGLADESHI CUISINE

Bangladeshi cuisine is a delightful culinary tradition that reflects the rich cultural heritage and diverse history of Bangladesh, a South Asian country located in the eastern part of the Indian subcontinent. The cuisine of Bangladesh is known for its distinct flavors, aromatic spices, and a harmonious blend of influences from various regions, including Persian, Mughal, and British.

What distinguishes Bangladeshi food from other cuisines, including that of West Bengal, India, with which it shares many similarities? How diversified and rich is it? What are the characteristics of our cuisine?

First, it's necessary to understand that a country's topography is one of the defining characteristics affecting its people's food. Because Bangladesh is a riverine country with many long-stretching paddy fields, the proverb "Mache bhaate Bengali" holds. Fish and rice are mainstays in Bangladeshi cuisine, and the average Bangladeshi household cannot live without them.

One thing to note about our traditional food is that it is delicious and nutritious. Whether it's the fish, the way rice is customarily prepared, the many vegetable dishes on the Bengali menu, or the proteins found in lentil soup or meat, the food of this region is unquestionably nourishing.

Fish, a popular Bengali dish, is, of course, quite healthful. Regarding nutrition, the method we typically prepare is ideal: "The water is not wasted away, allowing the cooked rice to retain the majority of its nutritious worth."

Bhorta is a popular rice-based dish. The sheer diversity of bhorta is incredible! An essential, easy-to-make everyday cuisine is made with mashed veggies or seafood, chilies, mustard oil, and salt. The 'daal' is always present on a Bangladeshi eating table (lentil soup).
Bangladeshi cuisine is centered on rice to a significant extent. Pitha, or rice cakes, is an excellent example of this principle. Pithas come in various flavors and are a favorite treat during Nabanna celebrations (rice harvest festivities) and throughout the winter.
Pitha is a Traditional dish. Several pithas' names and descriptions are in several Mymensingh ballards and other oral traditions. The following lines from Kajol-Rekha, a seventeenth-century poem, might be used as an example:

*"NANAJATI PITHA KAREY GANDHEY AMODITA
CHANDRAPULI KAREY KANYA CHANDRER AKRITA..."*

Many historical and literary works that have remained to this day describe our cuisine's uniqueness and variety. Looking at architectural and literary works suggestive of the concept that meat has been part of our diet, it is apparent that bengalis are not solely fish eaters or vegetarians." early bengali ate chicken and meat, according to excavations at mainamati and paharpur, as well as the ceramic ornamentation on kantajee mandir in dinajpur and the mangalkabya."

Fish, meat, and vegetables are prepared in various ways across bangladesh, owing to regional variances, which adds to the diversity of bangladeshi cuisine. The 'mezban' in chittagong is a feast, a large social gathering that features the unique 'mezbaani gosht,' an excellent beef curry served with plain rice.

Meanwhile, 'shatkora' is available in sylhet. "the meal of choice is the region's pride and joy, shatkora beef curry. Poncha (beef knuckle) khatta, a sour-tasting thick soup, is another well-known shatkora-based meal." cungga pitha is a sylheti specialty in which sticky rice is put inside young bamboo and smoked. The rice can be served either with thickened milk or fried.

Different ingredients and culinary methods around bangladesh, not just chittagong and sylhet, add to the varied gastronomy.

## LIST OF BANGLADESHI DISHES

Bangladeshi cuisine is known for its rich flavors, vibrant spices, and diverse dishes. It is heavily influenced by the culinary traditions of the Bengal region, which encompasses present-day Bangladesh and the Indian state of West Bengal. Here are some popular dishes and ingredients in Bangladeshi cuisine:

**Rice:** Rice is a staple food in Bangladesh, typically served with various curries and other dishes.

**Fish:** Bangladesh is known for its freshwater fish dishes. Hilsa, a type of fish, is particularly popular and is often cooked in a spicy mustard sauce called "shorshe ilish." Prawn and bhetki (Asian sea bass) are also commonly consumed.

**Meat curries:** Chicken, mutton, and beef are widely used in Bangladeshi cuisine. Curries made with these meats, such as chicken korma, mutton rezala, and beef bhuna, are popular.

**Vegetables:** Various vegetables are used in Bangladeshi cuisine, including potatoes, eggplants, okra, spinach, and gourds. Vegetarian dishes like shorshe bata diye begun (eggplant cooked in mustard paste) and aloo posto (potatoes cooked with poppy seeds) are well-known.

**Lentils and legumes:** Lentils, such as red lentils (masoor dal) and yellow split peas (chana dal), are commonly cooked and served with rice. Lentil-based soups, called dal, are an integral part of Bangladeshi meals.

**Bread:** Bangladeshi cuisine features a variety of bread, including traditional flatbreads like roti, paratha, and puri. Another famous bread is naan, which is typically served with kebabs or curries.

**Sweet dishes:** Bangladeshi desserts are often rich and sweet. Popular options include:
- Rasgulla (sweet cheese balls soaked in syrup).
- Shondesh (a sweet made from milk and sugar).
- Mishti doi (sweetened yogurt).
- 

**Street food:** Street food is a necessary part of Bangladeshi cuisine. Puchka (also known as golgappa or panipuri), fuchka (a variant of puchka), jhalmuri (a spicy puffed rice snack), and bhel puri (a savory snack made with puffed rice, vegetables, and chutneys) are popular street food items.

**Biriyani:** Bangladeshi biriyani is a flavorful rice dish cooked with aromatic spices, meat (such as chicken, mutton, or beef), and sometimes shrimp or fish. It is often embellished with fried onions and boiled eggs and served with raita (yogurt-based sauce) or a side salad.

**Kebabs:** Kebabs are famous in Bangladeshi cuisine, especially in street food stalls. Chicken tikka, seekh kebab (minced meat skewers), and shami kebab (spiced meat patties) are commonly enjoyed.

**Bhuna Khichuri:** Bhuna Khichuri, also known as khichuri or muri ghonto, is a hearty dish with rice, lentils, and vegetables. It is slow-cooked with spices, ghee (clarified butter) and often includes pieces of meat or fish.

**Shingara:** Shingara, similar to samosas, are deep-fried savory pastries filled with a spiced potato and vegetable mixture. They are commonly enjoyed as a tea-time snack or as street food.

**Chingri Malai Curry:** Chingri Malai Curry is a creamy and mildly spiced prawn curry made with coconut milk, turmeric, ginger, and other spices. It is a popular dish in coastal regions of Bangladesh.

**Shutki:** Shutki refers to dried fish, an essential ingredient in Bangladeshi cuisine. It is usually used to flavor various dishes, such as shutki bhorta (mashed dried fish with spices) or shutki shorshe (dried fish cooked in a mustard sauce).

**Pitha:** Pitha refers to traditional rice cakes or pancakes, typically made during festivals and special occasions. There are various types of pitha, including bhapa pitha (steamed rice cake), puli pitha (sweet rice dumplings), and chitoi pitha (deep-fried rice cakes).

**Borhani:** Borhani is a popular traditional drink in Bangladesh. It is a spiced yogurt-based beverage with mint, coriander, roasted cumin, and other spices. Borhani is often served during festive gatherings or as a refreshing drink.

**Haleem:** Haleem is a slow-cooked dish made with wheat, lentils, meat (usually beef or mutton), and spices. It has a thick and hearty texture, often enjoyed during the holy month of Ramadan or as a special dish during festive occasions.

**Kacchi Biryani:** Kacchi Biryani is a traditional and elaborate dish made with marinated meat (typically mutton or beef) and fragrant Basmati rice. The meat and rice are cooked concurrently in layers, giving the word a distinct flavor.

**Morog Polao:** Morog Polao is a flavorful rice dish cooked with chicken and aromatic spices. It is often garnished with fried onions, raisins, and cashews, adding a touch of sweetness and crunch to the dish.

**Chomchom:** Chomchom is a popular Bengali sweet made with cottage cheese (chenna) shaped into oval or cylindrical pieces and soaked in sugar syrup. It is often garnished with shredded coconut and enjoyed as a dessert.

**Luchi:** Luchi is a deep-fried, puffy bread made from all-purpose flour. It is similar to puri but is typically smaller in size. Luchi is commonly served with curries or enjoyed with chholar dal (Bengal gram lentil) for breakfast or special occasions.

**Mishti Pulao:** Mishti Pulao, also known as Sweet Pulao, is a fragrant rice dish cooked with aromatic spices, ghee, and raisins. It gets its sweetness from adding sugar or jaggery and is often served during festive celebrations.

**Jorda:** Jorda is a special rice dish prepared by flavoring cooked rice with ghee, sugar, and a hint of saffron. It is frequently served as a dessert or as part of celebratory meals.

**Mithai:** Mithai refers to various traditional sweets and desserts in Bangladeshi cuisine. Examples include:
- Roshogolla (soft cottage cheese balls soaked in sugar syrup).
- Sandesh (sweet made from milk and sugar).
- Malai cham (spongy sweet dipped in cream).

**Doi Maach:** Doi Maach is a famous Bengali fish curry made with fish (often freshwater fish like Rohu or Katla) cooked in a yogurt-based sauce. It has a creamy and tangy flavor.

**Shorshe Ilish:** Shorshe Ilish is a classic Bengali dish with Hilsa fish cooked in a mustard seed paste. It is a highly prized and beloved dish in Bangladeshi cuisine.

**Dhokar Dalna:** Dhokar Dalna is a vegetarian dish with lentil cakes (dhokar) steamed and then cooked in a spicy tomato-based gravy. It is often enjoyed with rice or flatbreads.

**Chitol Maacher Muitha:** Chitol Maacher Muitha is a unique dish made with minced fish (often from the Chital fish) mixed with spices, shaped into small balls, and cooked in a flavorful gravy.

**Bhapa Pitha:** Bhapa Pitha is a steamed rice cake made with rice flour, jaggery (a type of sugar), and grated coconut. It is a popular sweet dish enjoyed during festivals and special occasions.
Panta Bhat: Panta Bhat is a traditional dish with leftover cooked rice soaked overnight in water. It is served with fried Hilsa fish, pickles, and green chili.

**Shatkora Murgh:** Shatkora Murgh is a chicken curry made with Shatkora, a tangy and aromatic citrus fruit found in the Sylhet region of Bangladesh. The fruit adds a distinct and unique flavor to the dish.

**Kala Bhuna:** Kala Bhuna is a spicy and rich dish made with slow-cooked meat (often beef or mutton) in a thick gravy made from caramelized onions and a blend of spices. It is familiar for its deep, dark color and intense flavors.

These dishes and culinary elements add to the diverse and flavorful repertoire of Bangladeshi cuisine, showcasing unique ingredients, cooking techniques, and regional variations.

# MOST POPULAR FOOD

*Balish Misti*
Course: Dessert Producing region: Netrokona
**Description**: Balish Mishti (pillow sweet), so named for its pillow-like form and enormous size, has nearly a hundred years of tradition.

*Bograr Doi*
Course: Dessert Producing region: Bogra
**Description**: The most renowned variety of Mishti Doi in Bangladesh is made in Bogra, and the people of Bogra are famed for making the greatest Mishti Doi.

*Comilla Ras malai*
Course: Dessert Producing region: Comilla
**Description**: Ras malai, often known as rossomalai, is a dessert from the Indian subcontinent. Ras malai is made from sugary white cream or yellow-colored (flattened) balls of chhana soaked in cardamom-flavored malai (clotted cream). The greatest and oldest Rasmalai in Bangladesh was produced by "Matree Bhandar." It is a widely consumed sweet throughout the country.

*Chowk Bazaar Iftar*
Course: All courses Producing region: Old Dhaka
**Description**: During Ramadan, Chowk Bazaar is known for its Iftar products, which include Moghul cuisine and other traditional foods. For Holy Ramadan, about 500 distinct varieties of After are produced.

*Dhakai Bakarkhani*
Course: Entrée Producing region: Old Dhaka
**Description**: Bakarkhani or BaqarKhani, commonly known as Bakar Khani roti, is a thick, spicy flatbread from the Indian subcontinent's Mughlai cuisine. The traditional food/snack of the people of old

Dhaka, Dhakai Bakarkhani, is renowned for its quality and taste. Bakarkhani is typically served with tea.

### *Haji Biriyani*
Course: Main course Producing region: Old Dhaka
**Description**: Goat's flesh and seasoned rice are the main ingredients of Haji Biriyani (also known as Hajir Biriyani), a Chevon biryani dish. Some cheese may be added to this meal for additional flavor. The recipe calls for well-seasoned rice; chevon; mustard oil; garlic; onion; black pepper; cinnamon; clove; cardamom; salt; lemon; doi (yogurt); peanuts; cream; raisin; and some cheese (either cow or buffalo). The formula has been handed down from the restaurant's founder to his generation.

### *Kala bhuna*
Course: Main course Producing region: Chittagong
**Description**: Beef Kalo/Kala Bhuna is among Bangladesh's most popular beef meals. And the recipe's spices are the real star of the show. Traditional spices are used for cooking the beef shoulder as far as it is brown and tender. Chittagong is famous for its Kala buna and Mejbani Mangsho dishes.

### *Muktagachar monda*
Course: Dessert Producing region: Muktagachha, Mymensingh
**Description**: A classic sweetmeat, monda is made with walnuts and sugar. For its originality, taste, and taste, the sweet dates back to 1824 and is largely viewed in Bangladesh and many other countries.

### *Porabarir/Tangailer Chomchom*
Course: Dessert Producing region: Porabari, Tangail
**Description**: Chum, or Chom Chom as it's called in Bangladesh, is an old-fashioned Bengali sweet from Porabari. Dhaka and India are renowned for this dessert. The candy is brown and oval.

# BREAKFAST RECIPES

## BALUSHAHI RECIPE

Servings:4
Prep:15-20 min
Cook:30 min

**Ingredients**
- 1 and 1/2 cup of Flour
- 1/4 cup of Ghee
- 1/2 tsp Baking powder
- 1 cup of Sugar
- one pc Cardamom
- fry Oil

**Directions:**
Combine flour, a pinch of salt, baking powder, and ghee in a mixing bowl. Make a hard dough by gradually adding water. Refrain from overloading the dough by mixing it too much. Then, using your hands, separate the dough and re-mix it. To produce fluffy, repeat the method 6–7 times. Then split each piece in half and layer one over the other. To make more layers in Balushahi, repeat this process 3–4 times. Allow for a 5-minute rest period.

Combine the sugar, cardamom, and one cup of water in a pan. Bring the water to a boil. On a low-medium temperature, cook for 5 to 7 minutes. Then remove the remove from the heat and add the lemon juice. Set it aside for now.

The dough should now be sliced into tiny pieces. Make a circular and flatform using a bit of dough. Make a Balushahi-shaped hole inside the ball. Over low heat, fry them in a small amount of oil. Fry both sides until golden brown. Patience is required when frying them. Make sure the flame is manageable. It might take 13 to 15 minutes to fry a batch. Then keep away from the pan and place it on tissue paper to absorb any remaining oil.

Add them to the sugar syrup now. It's best if the syrup is a little warm. Keep turning and keeping them for 5 to 7 minutes. Then remove them. You may serve them now or cover them with mawa or milk powder.

Enjoy!

## SALTED ROUGH CRACKERS

Servings:6
Prep:20-25 min
Cook:30 min

**Ingredients**
- 1 cup of Wheat flour
- 1 tbsp Vegetable oil
- 1 tsp Black cumin
- 1/2 tsp  red chili powder
- 2 cups of Vegetable/soybean oil to fry
- As per requirement , water
- Salt

**Directions:**
In a bowl, combine wheat flour and baking powder. Mix in the salt, black cumin, red chili powder, and oil. To get a medium-soft dough, add some water. For 20 mins, cover the dough with a wet cloth. Knead enough dough for a few minutes, then slice it into tiny pieces and roll it into balls. Flatten a dough ball into a very thin bread, similar to rotis. Cut them into little pieces using a knife.

In a deep-frying pan, heat some oil. Add your crackers to the skillet and deep-fried them until golden and crispy. Drain the oil and spread it on a tissue to absorb the excess.

## NOLEN GURER CAKE

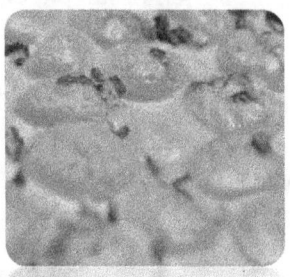

Servings:6
Prep:20 min
Cook:30

**Ingredients**
- 3 pcs Egg
- 1 cup of Flour
- 2 tbsp Cornflour
- 2 tbsp Milk powder
- 1 tsp Baking powder
- 1 cup of Jaggery
- 1/4 cup of Oil
- Salt

**Directions:**

To start, combine all dry ingredients, mix, and filter through a strainer. Set aside for now.
In a large mixing bowl, crack eggs at room temperature. If they were in the fridge, take them out and leave them outdoors for at least one hour. Now, beat the eggs using a hand beater or a hand whisk. When it turns into foam, add oil and beat well.
Mix in the melted jaggery with the dry ingredients well. Then add the egg to the combination of the dry ingredients. Gradually stir them in with a spatula or a spoon. Mix in a pinch of salt. At this step, do not overmix or use a hand mixer.
Grease a cake mold with oil or butter and line the bottom with parchment or regular paper. Fill it with a cake batter or cake mix. To remove bubbles, tap a few times.

Heat the oven to 350°F for 10 mins. Then bake your cake for 20 minutes at 160°C. Check with a toothpick after 20 minutes. When a toothpick put into the cake's middle comes out clean, it's done baking. If not, bake for another 5 mins. Before serving, remove them from the oven and allow them to cool fully.

## TELLER POA PITHA RECIPE

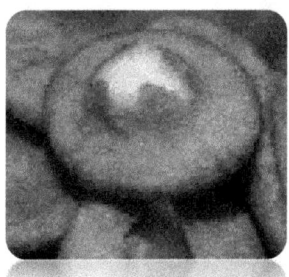

Servings:6
Prep:35-40 min
Cook:30 min

**Ingredients**
- 2 cups of Rice flour
- 1/2 cup of Wheat flour
- 3/4 cup of Jaggery
- 1/2 cup of liquid milk
- Salt
- Oil

**Directions:**
Combine rice flour, all-purpose wheat flour, salt, jaggery, and melted milk in a mixing bowl. Everything should be well mixed. Make a smooth batter by gradually adding warm water. Whisk the batter for 2-3 minutes or until completely smooth. To enable flavors to meld, cover and put away for 30 minutes. To make air bubbles, whisk the mixture for 5 minutes after 30 minutes.

In a depth pan, heat the oil. To start, heat the oil over a medium flame. Then reduce heat to low and drop a tablespoon batter into the hot oil. Allow it to rise and puff up after that. Tap the oil with a spoon or spatula to get it to the top. Then cook both sides until golden brown and crispy.

When completed, filter the oil and put it on tissue paper to absorb any extra oil. After that, serve.

# MINI MOGLAI POROTA RECIPE

Servings:2
Prep:30-35 min
Cook:20 min

**Ingredients**
- 1 cup of Wheat flour
- 1 pc Egg
- 1/2 cup of Chopped onion
- 1 tsp Chopped green chili
- 1 tbsp Coriander leaves
- 1/2 tsp Roasted cumin powder
- Oil
- Salt

**Directions:**

Combine flour, salt, and 1 tsp oil in a mixing bowl. With your hand, gently combine them. Add water to get a smooth, flexible dough for a few minutes, and knead it until it's smooth. Spray the dough with oil, cover, and set aside for 30 minutes.

And meanwhile, prepare the egg staffing. Chilies, onion, coriander leaves, cumin powder, salt, and egg should all be combined in a bowl. Set it aside for now.
Cut the dough into six equal pieces now. Please take all of the pieces and roll them into balls by hand one by one. Make a ball and flatten it to the thinnest feasible thickness. Place some egg filling in the center and seal it like a paratha by extending the borders towards the center.

In a depth pan, heat the oil. Gently place mini parathas in it and fry one side till golden. Then, on medium-low heat, turn it and cook both sides until golden. Then keep them away from the pan and add them on tissue paper to soak any leftover oil before serving warm with sliced cucumber, onion, and ketchup or sauce.

## DAL PURI RECIPE

**Ingredients**

- 1/2 cup of Lentil
- 5 pcs Fried red chili
- Salt
- 1 & 1/2 cup of Flour
- For deep frying Vegetable oil
- 1 tbsp Vegetable oil
- Turmeric powder
- Water

**Directions:**

Combine flour, salt, and oil in a large mixing bowl. Hand-mix the ingredients. Now gradually add room-temperature water and knead for 5-7 minutes to form a soft dough. Then brush the dough with oil and set it aside to rest for 30 minutes.
Meanwhile, cook the lentils with a sprinkle of turmeric powder and salt until the water evaporates. Set aside the lentil, including the crushed shallow-fried red chilies and optionally chopped coriander leaves.
Take the dough after 30 minutes and cut it up. Take half part of the dough, knead it for 3-4mins to give it a long form, then slices it into

little pieces with a knife. Make balls out of small bits of dough. Take those balls and flatten them with your hands before filling them with the lentil mixture. Close the holes and squeeze them into lenticular forms using your hands. Oil a flat surface and use a roller to flatten them into "Puri" forms.

On medium-low heat, heat oil in a deep frying pan. If using a large pan, add the Puries one at a time and keep pressing them down into the oil with a spatula or colander. When they swallow, flip them over and cook both sides until golden brown. Remove them from the oil using a sieve and absorb any excess oil with kitchen tissue. To get more flavor and taste of the Puries, sprinkle some black salt powder. Serve immediately with a salad and your favorite sauce.

## PIZZA RECIPE WITHOUT OVEN

Servings:3-4
Prep:25 min
Cook:30 min

**Ingredients**
- 1 cup of Flour
- 1 tsp Sugar
- 1 tsp Instant dry yeast
- 2 tbsp Oil
- Tomato sauce
- Grated cheese
- Capsicum
- Chopped onion
- Sausage
- As required, Mixed herbs
- Chili flakes

- Salt

**Directions:**
Take a big mixing bowl. Combine the flour, sugar, salt, and yeast in a bowl and mix. Mix all the dry components in a sizeable bowl and begin mixing. Then add lukewarm liquid milk gradually to produce a soft dough. Include the oil and knead the dough for another 2 to 3 minutes. Allow yeast to activate for 2 hours by covering and setting away. The whole dough will have doubled in size in just two hours. Knead the dough one more. With your hands, stretch and fold into the inside. Please put it on the frying pan and flatten it with your hands until it's the size you want it to be with a typical pizza shape.

To minimize extra bubbles, puncture several holes on the surface with a fork. Cover and bake for 5 minutes on one side over very low heat. Then bake for another 5 minutes on the other side. Now flip it over and top it with tomato sauce, cheese, sausage, onion, capsicum, or any other toppings you choose. Cook, covered until everything is well cooked, and the cheeses have melted. Then slice into pieces and serve while still warm.

# DOUGH PARATHA RECIPE

Servings:2
Prep:15-17 min
Cook:20 min

**Ingredients**
- 1 cup of Wheat flour
- 1 tbsp Milk powder
- 1/2 tsp Sugar
- Salt
- Oil

**Directions:**

Combine all-purpose flour, sugar, salt, and milk powder in a mixing bowl. Make a smooth batter by gradually including water. Whisk the batter for 2-3 minutes or until completely smooth. Cover and place aside for 5 minutes to allow flavors to meld.

Brush oil all over a pan that has been heated. Pour in a little amount of batter and lower the heat. Cut the roti into a circle. Next, let it cook for a few minutes on one side.

When it's done, turn it over and finish cooking the other side. Then keep away from the pan and put on tissue paper to absorb any remaining oil. After that, serve.

# FRIED LENTIL PATTIES RECIPE

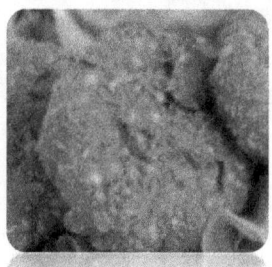

**Ingredients**
- 1 cup of Lentils
- 1 cup of Chopped onion
- 1 tbsp Chopped green chili
- 1 tsp Cumin powder
- 1/2 tsp Tumeric powder
- 1 tsp of every Ginger-garlic paste
- Salt
- To fry Vegetable oil

**Directions:**
Soak lentils for an hour in water. Lentils should be thoroughly washed and dried. Mix the lentils in a blender until they are as smooth as possible. While blending, do not use any water. Add the ginger-garlic paste, onions, green chilies, cumin powder, turmeric powder, and salt. Mix everything up thoroughly with your hands, then set it aside.

In a deep fryer, heat some oil. To cook, make little pellets from the lentil mixture and drop them into the heated oil. While frying, keep the flame on medium-high. For a minute, fry it. Then flip it finely and cook for an extra minute on the other side.

Remove from the oil using a strainer after both sides have become reddish-brown and seem crispy. To soak up the extra oil, place them on a kitchen tissue. To experience the crispiness, serve warm.

# MALTOVA CAKE RECIPE

Servings: 6
Prep: 30 min
Cook: 45 min

**Ingredients**
- 3 pcs Egg
- 3/4 cup of Wheat flour
- 1/2 cup of Malkova
- 1 tsp Baking powder
- 1/2 cup of Sugar
- 1/2 cup of Vegetable/soybean oil
- 1/2 tsp Vanilla essence
- You can add Dry fruits (Nuts, raisins, confiture, etc.)

**Directions:**
Except for the dry nuts, sift the dry ingredients through a strainer. Combine the egg and sugar in a sizeable bowl and whisk until smooth. Now add the oil and continue to beat for a few minutes. Gradually incorporate the dry ingredients while continuing to beat. Pour in the vanilla extract. Stop pounding when everything is thoroughly combined and the batter is smooth. Now combine the dry nuts with the rest of the ingredients.

First, grease the cake mold with oil, then sprinkle it with flour. Fill the mold half with batter and tap it to eliminate air bubbles.

Cook for 40-50 minutes at 170°C in a preheated oven. Set a plate stand inside a heavy pan and place the cake mold on that stand to bake on the heat. Bake for 50 minutes on low heat with the cover on the pan. When you're finished, poke the cake with a toothpick to see if it's done. You understand the cake is made baking when a toothpick in the middle comes out fully clean. If it comes out too wet, bake it for 4-5 mins to dry it out.

# EASY CUPCAKE RECIPE

Servings:1
Prep:10 min Cook:2 min

**Ingredients**
*(CHOCOLATE CAKE)*
- 3 tbsp Wheat flour
- 2 tbsp Sugar
- 2 tbsp Vegetable oil
- 1 tbsp Cocoa powder
- 3 tbsp Liquid milk
- 1/4 tsp Baking powder
- Baking soda
- 1 tsp Chocolate chips

*(VANILLA CAKE)*
- 3 tbsp Wheat flour
- 2 tbsp Sugar
- 3 tbsp Liquid milk
- 1/4 tsp Vanilla essence
- 1/4 tsp Baking powder
- Just a pinch of Baking soda

**Directions:**
Taking a cup that can be reheated fork is a great tool to combine the contents thoroughly. There should be no irregularities in the final piece.
Cook it for 2 minutes in the oven. Using a toothpick, make sure everything is in order. Bake for another minute if the toothpick comes out clean. If it's clean, it's prepared to consume.
The cake will be dry if it is overbaked.

# CHIRA CHOP RECIPE

Servings:4
Prep:15-17 min
Cook:20 min

**Ingredients**
- 1/2 cup of Flatten rice
- 1/3 cup of Chopped onion
- 1 tsp Chopped green chilies
- 1/2 tsp Roasted cumin powder
- 1/2 tsp Roasted coriander powder
- 1/4 tsp Turmeric powder
- 1/4 tsp Red chili powder
- As needed Salt
- To fry Oil

**Directions:**
The rice should be cleaned and soaked for 30 minutes. Then drain completely. In a sizable bowl, combine all the ingredients except the oil. Now you can use your hands to combine the ingredients. If necessary, a water molecule can be added. Mix everything up thoroughly and form it into cutlets or chops. On a medium burner, heat oil in a pan for frying. Cook the chops carefully and patiently on medium-low heat until golden brown. When they're done, squeeze them out of the oil and apply them on a tissue to absorb any extra oil. Serve hot with ketchup.

# PAV BREAD RECIPE

Servings:4
Prep:2 hr 35 min
Cook:25 min

**Ingredients**
- 1.5 cups of Flour
- 2 tbsp Milk powder
- 1/2 tbsp dry yeast
- 1/2 tbsp to 1 tbsp Sugar
- 1 tsp Salt
- one pc Beaten egg
- 1/2 cup of melted butter

**Directions:**
Take a big mixing bowl. Combine flour, milk powder, sugar, salt, and yeast in a bowl and mix. In a sizeable bowl, whisk to combine the ingredients until smooth. Then, add the beaten eggs and the butter and mix thoroughly. Make a soft dough by gradually adding lukewarm liquid milk. For another 2 to 3 mins, continue to knead the dough once you've added the butter. Allow yeast to activate by covering and setting aside for 2 hours.

After around two hours, the dough will have more than doubled. Knead the dough one more. With your hands, stretch and fold into the interior. Please put it on the tray and flatten it into a circular shape with your hands. Cut into nine pieces that are all the same size.

Bake the dough balls, which have been formed into small balls, on a baking sheet. Allow them to rise for 20 minutes under cover. Then brush the top with a cracked egg.

Heat the oven to 160 °F for 10 minutes. Heat a big pan on high heat for 15-17 minutes in the oven if you wish to bake with gas induction. Make a position for oneself. Put the tray on the stand and bake for 20-25 mins on low heat. Take them out when everything is great. Allow cooling slightly before serving heated.

# MILK CHOCOLATE CAKE RECIPE

Servings:6
Prep:20-25 min
Cook:30 min

**Ingredients**
- 2 pcs Egg
- 1 cup of Flour
- 1/4 cup of Cocoa powder
- 1 tbsp Milk powder
- 1 tsp Baking powder
- 1/4 tsp Baking soda
- 3/4 cup of Sugar
- 2 tbsp Oil
- 1 tsp Vanilla essence
- 1 tbsp Butter
- 1/2 cup of liquid milk

**Directions:**

To begin, combine all dry ingredients, mix, and filter through a strainer. Set aside for now.

Put eggs at room temp, sugar, oil, and vanilla extract in a blender jug. Blend for 2-4 minutes or until the sugar has melted. Stop combining when the mixture becomes frothy and fluffy.

In a sizeable bowl, combine the dry components and toss well. Then add the egg mixture slowly and gently using a spatula or whisk. Refrain from over-mixing the ingredients.

In a pan, bring the milk and butter to a boil. Then, gradually incorporate this into the cake batter with a spatula or whisk.

Using oil or butter, grease a cake mold. Put a single piece of baking paper at the bottom of the container. Pour in the cake mix/batter and tap it twice to eliminate air bubbles.

For 5 minutes, preheat a pan with a cover. Then set up a stand and lay the cake mold inside. With the cover on, bake on a very low burner for 40-45 minutes. Preheat your oven for 10 minutes if you want to bake. Then bake your cake for 25-30 minutes at 160°C.

Check with a toothpick after 45 minutes. The cake is ready to serve if a toothpick comes out clean. If not, bake for another 5 minutes. The same method works in the oven. Then remove the mold and set it aside to cool thoroughly. Remove the mold with a knife or a spoon. Slice into your preferred size pieces and serve.

## FULKO LUCHI RECIPE

Servings:5
Prep:35-40 min
Cook:20 min

**Ingredients**
- 1 cup of Flour
- 1/2 tsp Sugar
- Salt
- 1 & 1/2 cup vegetable oil

**Directions:**
Combine flour, salt, sugar, and two tablespoons of oil in a mixing bowl. Combine all of the ingredients well. You may get a soft, smooth, and ideal dough by gradually adding water and kneading for 5-10 minutes. A small amount of oil should coat the dough before putting it in the fridge. Cut the dough into tiny pieces and use your hands to shape every piece into a small ball. Flatten the balls with a roller on a level surface after dusting some flour. Instead of flour, you may use oil. They shouldn't be overly thick or too thin.
In a deep fry pan, heat enough oil to deep fry over high heat. Heating the oil to a high temp is critical for a fluffy effect. Add the bread one by one to the oil and press them down with a spatula or a spud until they form a ball shape. Fry the other portions till it is golden brown. They will turn hard or crispy if you cook them for too long. Before serving, squeeze off any excess oil with a filter and sweep away any remaining oil with kitchen tissue. Serve with meat or vegetables while still warm.

# HANDI KEBAB

Servings: 5
Prep: 10-15 min
Cook: 20 min

**Ingredients**
- 300 gm Beef/mutton
- 1 tbsp Onion paste
- 1 tsp of every Ginger-garlic paste
- 2 tbsp Papaya paste
- 1/2 cup of sour yogurt
- 1/2 tsp Nutmeg-mace paste
- 1 tsp Tomato sauce
- 1/2 tsp Cardamom powder
- 1/2 tsp Coriander powder
- 1 tsp Cumin powder
- 1 tbsp Red chili powder
- 4 tbsp Vegetable oil
- 3-4 pcs Cinnamon
- 3-4 pcs Cloves
- 2 pcs Bay leaves
- Salt

**Directions:**

Cut the meat into thin, long pieces, then wash thoroughly and drain it. Make sure the meat doesn't have water in it.

In a mixing bowl, place the meat. Including two tablespoons of oil, combine everything in a large bowl. Combine all of the ingredients well. After covering, refrigerate for at least 6 or 24 hours. The longer you marinate, the more flavor and juiciness you'll get. In a pan on high flame, heat the remaining oil. Stir in the bay leaves a little. Continue to stir in the marinated meat. With the cover on, cook for 5 to 10 minutes. There's no need to add water at this point. The meat begins to release water as it cooks. Cook the meat in the released water until it has dried to half its original volume.

When the water evaporates, and the oil begins to release, add 1/2 cup of water and cook on medium-high heat up to the meat is tender. If necessary, you can add extra water. When it's done, keep stirring until it's charred and looks like a kebab. While warm, serve with naan, roti, paratha, pulao, or biryani.

# EGG PIZZA SANDWICH RECIPE

Servings:2
Prep:10-15 min
Cook:10 min

**Ingredients**
- 1 pc Egg
- 4 pcs Bread slices
- As required, Grated cheese
- Chopped sweet chili/capsicum/tomato
- Chili flakes
- Oregano-parsley
- Butter
- Salt

**Directions:**

In a sizeable pan, heat one tablespoon of butter. Add one egg to the fry, whisked with a pinch of salt. Make an egg scramble. After that, set it away.

Melt some butter in the same pan over low heat. 2 bread pieces are added, and both sides of the bread slices are lightly toasted. Then, on top of a bread piece, spread scrambled eggs, chopped sweet chili/capsicum/cucumber/tomato, grated cheese, chili flakes, oregano, and parsley (Italian herbs).

On top of that, place a fresh slice of bread and firmly press it down. Snew both sides until the cheese has melted. When done, please remove it from the fire and slice it into sandwich shapes. Serve with tomato ketchup on the side.

# STICK KEBAB RECIPE

Servings:4
Prep:15-20 min Cook:15 min

## Ingredients

- 250 gm Boneless beef/ chicken
- 1 tbsp Onion paste
- 1 tsp Ginger-garlic paste
- 1/2 tsp Cumin powder
- 1 tsp Red chili powder
- 1/2 tsp every Cardamom-cinnamon powder
- 1 tsp Kabab masala
- 1 tbsp Vegetable
- 1 tsp Butter
- bamboo sticks
- Salt

## Directions:

Slice the beef, mutton, or chicken into thin slices. Drain and wash thoroughly. To absorb extra moisture, use tissue paper.
Please put them in a bowl now. Mix onion, ginger, garlic paste, cumin powder, red chili powder, cinnamon powder, cardamom powder, and salt in a mixing bowl. With your hands, especially directly, all of the components. Then chill it for 8 hours in the usual chamber of a refrigerator. They can be frozen for up to 15 days. Take them out from the freezer 30 mins before cooking to allow them to thaw.
Take several kabab sticks, which are made of wood or bamboo. Soak them for 30 minutes in water. Then, using the stick, insert the meat pieces.
In a sizeable pan, heat the oil and butter. Cook for 5 minutes on one side over low heat. When one side is complete, turn it over and cook for 5 mins on the other side. Your kabab is ready to eat. Serve with onion slices with roti, paratha, naan, or pilaf rice.

# EGGPLANT FRITTERS RECIPE

Servings:6
Prep:15-20 min Cook:20 min

**Ingredients**
- one pc Brinjal/eggplant
- 1 cup of Gram flour
- 1 tbsp Rice flour
- 1 tbsp Cornflour
- 1/2 tsp Ginger paste
- 1/2 tsp Garlic paste
- 1/2 tsp Roasted cumin powder
- 1/2 tsp Roasted coriander powder
- 1 tsp Dried red chili powder
- To deep-fry Vegetable oil
- As needed Salt
- 1 tsp Vegetable oil

**Directions:**
Wash and cut the eggplant in half or quarters, then thinly slice each piece. Please ensure they're thin enough to cook thoroughly without collecting too much oil during frying.
Mix the gram flour, rice flour, cornflour, garlic-ginger paste, roasted cumin powder, roasted coriander powder, dried red chili powder, salt, and oil to make the batter. Now gradually add room-temperature water to form a soft paste that is neither too thick nor too thin.
In a medium-sized pan, heat the oil. Take a slice, dip it in the batter, and deep fry it with 3-4 other pieces in the oil. When it swells, use a spatula or a spoon to pour heated oil on them. Both sides get fluffy and crispy as a result of this technique. Fry the opposite side as well. Long, moderate heat should fry the slices until they get dark or reddish and crispy eggplant/beguni. After they've been fried, strain them out of the oil and place them on kitchen napkins to soak up any excess oil. Serve hot with chili powder and black salt on top for more flavor.

# CRISPY EGG BALL RECIPE

Servings:4
Prep:15-20 min Cook:20 min

**Ingredients**
- 2 pcs Grated boiled eggs
- 1 tbsp Finely chopped onion
- 1 tsp Chopped green chilies
- 1 tsp Chopped coriander leaves
- 1 tbsp Chopped capsicum
- Salt
- 1/2 tsp Roasted coriander powder
- 1/2 tsp Roasted cumin powder
- 1 tbsp Cornflour
- 1 tbsp Gram flour
- 1/2 tsp Red chili powder
- A pinch of mixed herbs
- Oil

**Directions:**
Mix all ingredients (except oil) in a mixing bowl. Now use your hands to combine the contents. Then take a few and roll them into little balls. In a bowl, 2 tsp flour, a pinch of salt, red chili powder, and a little water. Mix all the components in a bowl to make a thin batter. Place the breadcrumbs in a separate bowl. To make the egg balls, dip them in the flour batter, then coat them with breadcrumbs. Set aside for now. Carry on in the same pocudure with the remaining components. On medium heat, heat cooking oil in a pan for frying. Fry them carefully and patiently over medium-low heat until they are golden brown. When they're done, squeeze them out of the oil and apply them on a tissue to absorb any extra oil. Serve warm with the ketchup or chutney of your choice.

# SEMOLINA SUJIR BISCUIT PITHA RECIPE

Servings:4
Prep:15-17 min
Cook:20 min

**Ingredients**
- 1 cup of Semolina
- 2 tbsp Milk powder
- 1/2 cup of Sugar
- 1/4 tsp Salt
- 1 tsp Ghee
- To fry Oil

**Directions:**

Combine the egg, sugar, salt, and ghee in a mixing bowl. Beat until the sugar has melted. Toss in the semolina and milk powder now (optionally add cardamom powder or vanilla for flavor). Mix everything up thoroughly with your hands and set aside for 5 minutes. Take some and form them into a little chop or biscuit. Heat oil in a sizeable pan on a regular flame for deep frying. Fry both sides gently and carefully on low heat until brown and crispy. When done, strain them out of the oil and place them on a tissue to absorb any extra oil. Serve hot or reserve in an airtight container for up to 2 days.

# CRISPY PIYAJU RECIPE

**Ingredients**
- 1 cup of Mixed dals
- 1 cup of Chopped onion
- 2 tbsp Chopped green chilies
- Salt
- 1/2 tsp Turmeric powder
- Oil

**Directions:**
Combine the dals in a bowl and mix. Soak for 4 hours in water. Drain well after a deep clean with clean water.
Blend the dals in a blender until they are almost paste-like. While blending, do not use any water. Add the chopped onions, green

chilies, turmeric powder, and salt at this stage. Mix everything up thoroughly with your hands, then set it aside.

In a deep fry pan, heat enough oil to deep fry. Take some dal mixtures, flatten them into a tiny piyaju form, and cook it in hot oil. While frying, keep the flame on medium-high. Flip once during the cooking process to ensure even browning on both sides.

Remove from the oil using a strainer after both sides have become reddish-brown and seem crispy. To soak up the extra oil, place them on a kitchen tissue. To experience the crispiness, serve warm.

## SAUTEED BUTTER GARLIC MUSHROOMS RECIPE

Servings:3-4
Prep:15-20 min Cook:10 min

**Ingredients**
- 1 Canned can think of mushroom
- 2 tbsp Butter
- 2 tsp Chopped garlic
- 1/2 tsp Chili flakes
- 1/2 cup of Chopped onion
- 1/2 tsp Soy sauce
- 1 tsp Tomato sauce
- 1/4 tsp Black pepper powder
- Salt
- 1/2 tsp Lemon juice

**Directions:**
First, properly clean the mushroom with water and allow it to drain. Cut into smaller pieces.

Now melt the butter in a pan. Then include the chopped garlic and chili flakes and cook until golden brown. After that, throw in a big chopped onion. For a bit, stir to cook. Add the mushroom and salt, and stir for 2 to 5 minutes or until the mushroom is cooked thoroughly. Stir in the soy sauce for a few minutes.

Now add the tomato sauce and black pepper powder. Complete with a squeeze of lemon juice for a finishing touch. If preferred, a few chopped coriander leaves can be sprinkled on top. Warm noodles or fried rice are a good complement.

## VANILLA CUP OF CAKE RECIPE

Servings:6
Prep:15-20 min Cook:30 min

**Ingredients**
- 1/2 cup of Flour
- 1/2 cup of Sugar
- 2 tbsp Powder milk
- Two pcs Eggs
- 2 tbsp Oil
- 1/2 tsp Baking powder
- 1/2 tsp Vanilla essence

**Directions:**
Combine all dry ingredients, mix, and filter through a strainer. Set aside for now.
In a large mixing bowl, break eggs at room temperature. If they were in the fridge, take them out and leave them outside for at least one hour. Now, beat the eggs using a hand beater or a hand whisk. Gradually add icing sugar/sugar and mix thoroughly when it becomes foam. After that, mix in the vanilla extract and the oil (or melted butter).
Now add the dry ingredients mixture. Gradually stir them in with a spatula or a spoon. At this step, do not overmix or use a hand blender. Grease a cake mold with oil or butter and line the bottom with parchment or regular paper. Cover it with a cake batter or cake mix. To remove bubbles, tap a few times. Heat the oven to 350°F for 10 mins. Then bake your cake for 20 minutes at 160°C. Check with a toothpick after 20 minutes. When a toothpick in the cake's center comes out clean, it's done baking. If not, bake for another 5 minutes. Allow them to cool entirely once they've finished baking before eating.

# CHICKPEA RECIPE

Servings:4
Prep:10 min Cook:40

**Ingredients**
- 500 gm Chickpeas
- 1/2 cup of Chopped onion
- 4/5 pcs Garlic cloves
- 6/7 pcs Green chilies
- 1 tsp Turmeric powder
- 1/2 cup of Oil
- Salt
- one medium in size Potato

**Directions:**

Soak chickpeas for at least 4 to 8 hours after washing them. You may soak it overnight. Then repeat the process and thoroughly drain. In a pressure cooker, heat two tablespoons of vegetable/soybean oil. An alternative is to use a pan. However, cooking effectively in a pressure cooker takes less time. Then add the soaked chickpeas, onion, garlic, sliced chilies, turmeric powder, salt, and water to the pot. Up to 6–8 whistles can be cooked.

After adding the chopped potatoes, cook for 3 -4 whistles on medium heat. Chickpeas must be cooked to perfection. Include oil and chopped onion in a pan now. Fry until the color changes to a brown color. Cook for 2 to 5 minutes with chickpeas in it.

Now it's time to serve; the amount of ingredients you use is entirely up to you and your preferences. In a mixing bowl, mix the cooked chickpeas. It's time to add the cucumber, tomato, coriander leaves, green chile, and onion, and serve. Before eating, squeeze a fresh lemon over everything and combine well. It will, without a doubt, offer more taste and flavor.

# CRISPY VAJA PULI PITHA RECIPE

Servings:5-6
Prep:30 min Cook:20 min

**Ingredients**
- 1 and 1/2 cups of shredded coconut
- 1/2 cup of Sugar
- 2 pcs Cinnamon
- one pc Cardamom
- 1 cup of Rice flour
- 1/2 cup of Wheat flour
- Oil

**Directions:**
Cook coconut, sugar, cardamom, and cinnamon in a frypan over low heat till the sugar has dissolved and the mix is sticky. Please switch off the heat and wait for it to cool.

Combine 1 & 1/2 cup water and 1 tsp salt in a small saucepan. Bring the water to a boil. Cover with the lid after adding the rice flour and wheat flour. Cook for 5-7 mins on a medium-low flame. Now, using a spoon, combine everything. Please enable it to cool for a few minutes. Then knead the dough up to it is soft and smooth. If necessary, you can sprinkle normal-temperature water.

Take half part of the dough, knead it for 3-4 mins to give it a long form, then cut it into little pieces with a knife. Make balls out of little bits of dough. Take those balls and flatten them with your hands before filling them with the coconut mixture. Close the holes and press them with your hands to make a lenticular form or any shape you like. To keep, put them in a zip-lock bag in the refrigerator.

On medium-low heat, heat oil in a deep frying pan. One by one, add the pithas. Flip once during the cooking process to ensure even browning on both sides. Every batch may take 7 to 10 minutes to cook to perfection. Using a sieve, take them from the oil and absorb any excess oil with kitchen tissue. Then allow cooling before dishing.

# BUTTER COOKIE RECIPE

Servings:4
Prep:20-25 min Cook:30 min

**Ingredients**
- 1/2 cup of Salted Butter
- 1/2 cup of Powdered sugar
- one pc Egg yolk
- 1/2 tsp Vanilla extract
- 1 cup of Wheat flour
- 2 tbsp Cornflour
- 2 tbsp Milk powder
- 1 tsp Baking powder

**Directions:**

Take a bowl and pour it into it. Mix the butter and blended sugar in a mixing bowl. Using a spoon or a whisk, thoroughly combine the contents. Combine the egg yolk and vanilla essence in a bowl and mix. Mix well with cornflour, milk powder, flour, and baking powder in a strainer.
Knead the dough and cut it into tiny pieces. Make little balls and flatten them to bake muffins or cookies. You may use a fork or a toothpick to make a basic design for them.
Brush a baking pan with butter before putting it in the oven. Arrange the biscuits on top of it. Preheat the oven or the cooking pan of your choosing.
Bake at 160°C for 15-20 minutes in the oven or 25-30 minutes on very low heat in a pan with a stand. Then keep them away from the oven and allow them to cool fully. You may eat it immediately or keep it in an airtight container for up to 12-15 days.

# NARKEL NARU RECIPE

Servings:3-4
Prep:15-20 min Cook:20 min

**Ingredients**
- 1 and 1/2 cups of shredded coconut
- 1 cup of Sugarcane jaggery
- 1/4 tsp Cardamom powder

**Directions:**
Put the coconut, jaggery, and cardamom in a frying pan and stir everything together with your hands until the jaggery is completely dissolved.
Now, turn on the flame and patiently cook on medium-high heat. Continue swirling until the mixture becomes sticky. Reduce the heat to low and transfer to a bowl to cool.
Add a small amount of oil or ghee to your hands. Refrain from overworking the ingredients by making large balls out of a small amount. If they get cold, it will be challenging to form them. Then set them aside to cool completely. They can be kept at normal temperature for up to 5 days or a week.

# EGG SANDWICH

Servings-2-3
Prep:10 min Cook:20 min

**Ingredients**
- 8 pcs Bread slices
- 2 pcs Hard-boiled eggs
- 1 tbsp Chopped onion
- 1/2 tsp Chopped green chilies
- 2 tbsp Chopped cucumber
- 1 tbsp Tomato sauce
- 2 tbsp Mayonnaise
- 1/4 cup of Butter
- Salt

**Directions:**

Using a fork, mash two hard-boiled eggs. Combine the onion, green chilies, mayonnaise, tomato sauce, cucumber, and salt in a sizeable bowl and mix. Combine all of the ingredients well. Set it aside for now.

Now, in a pan, melt some butter and fry it up. Both sides of the bread pieces should be lightly browned. Then pour the egg mixer over the bread and smooth it out evenly.

Now add a slice of cheese. Make sure the cheese is melted by toasting a 2nd piece of bread on top of it. When done, please remove it from the fire and cut it into sandwich shapes. Warm the meal for serving.

## POTATO CHEESE BALLS

Servings:4
Prep:15-17 min Cook:20 min

**Ingredients**
- 1 cup of Boiled potato
- 1 tbsp Chopped onion
- 1/2 tsp Chopped green chilies
- 1 tbsp Chopped coriander leaves
- 1/4 tsp Chili flakes
- 1/4 tsp Black pepper powder
- 2 tbsp Grated cheese
- 1/4 tsp Italian mixed herbs
- 1 tsp Salt
- Oil

**Directions:**

Except for the oil, put all the ingredients in a mixing bowl. The next part is to use your hands to combine the ingredients. If necessary, a small amount of water can be added. Then take a few and roll them into little balls.

2 tsp flour, a teaspoon of salt, a small amount of red chili powder, and a little water in a bowl. Mix all the components in a bowl to

make a thin batter. Place the breadcrumbs in a separate bowl. To make the egg balls, dip them in the flour batter, then coat them with breadcrumbs. Set aside for now. Carry on in the same procedure with the remaining components.

On a medium burner, heat oil in a pan for deep frying. Fry them carefully and patiently over medium-low heat until they are golden brown. When they're done, squeeze them out of the oil and apply them on a tissue to absorb any extra oil. Serve warm with the ketchup or chutney of your choice.

## EGG SALAD RECIPE

Servings:2
Prep:10-15 min Cook:10 min

### Ingredients

- two pcs eggs
- one pc Cucumber
- 1 pc Tomato
- 2 tbsp Chopped onion
- one pc Chopped green chili
- 1 tbsp Chopped coriander leaves
- 2 tbsp Lemon juice
- 1 tbsp Olive oil
- 1 tbsp Mayonnaise
- 1/2 tbsp Black pepper powder
- Salt
- 1/2 cup of Cabbage

### Directions:

Cut veggies and eggs into your preferred shapes. If using cabbage, season it with salt and set it aside for two minutes. Then press hard to expel the water.

It's now time to create the dressing. Mix olive oil, mayonnaise, pepper powder, salt, sugar, and lemon juice in a mixing bowl.

Now add the veggies and stir thoroughly. Then add the eggs and gently fold them in. After combining, serve as quickly as possible. If you reserve it too long, it will turn soggy.

# RICE RECIPES

## SWEET RICE RECIPE

**Ingredients**
- 2 cup ofs of Aromatic rice (Kalojeera/Chinigura)
- 1 cup of Sugar
- 2 pcs Bay leaves
- 2 pcs Cinnamon
- 5-6 pcs Cloves
- 1/2 tsp Cardamom powder
- 1/2 cup of Ghee
- Dry fruits (Nuts)
- Confiture (Morobba)
- 1 tsp Food color

**Directions:**
Rice should be carefully washed, soaked in water for ten minutes, and then thoroughly drained.

Pour enough water and 1 tsp of soybean/vegetable oil into a big pan. Boil things down to a simmer. When the water comes to a boil, include the rice and cook for six more minutes. The rice should absorb seventy percent of the water before it is done. Discard the water. This time, there's no need to use cold water to wash the rice.

Turn on the burner and add 1/2 cup water, sugar, and milk to a pan. When the sugar has dissolved and is beginning to boil, turn the heat up and add cardamom powder, cinnamon, cloves, and bay leaves. While it's heating up, stir in the rice. Distribute the ingredients equally using a spatula. Cook, covered, for 7 minutes on medium-low heat.

Rice should be placed on the dried fruits, confiture, or murabba (if desired). Cook for a further five minutes at a low temperature. Then, turn off the heat. Place the cover on the pot, add 1 tsp ghee, and let it sit for 5 minutes. You may now offer your sweet rice to your guests.

# VUNA KHICHURI RECIPE

**Ingredients**
- 500 gm Normal rice
- 200 gm Chickpea dal
- 1/2 cup of Vegetable
- 2 tbsp Ghee
- 1/2 tsp Black cumin
- 2 pcs Bay leaves
- four pcs of every Whole cinnamon & cardamom
- 1/2 cup of Chopped onion
- 1 tbsp of every Garlic-ginger paste
- 1 tsp Cumin powder
- 1 tsp Turmeric powder
- 4-5 pcs Whole green chilies
- 1 tbsp Dried red chili powder
- Crispy fried onion
- Salt
- 4 pcs Cloves
- 5-6 pcs Black pepper
- 1/2 tsp Nutmeg-mace paste

**Directions:**

Chickpeas should be washed and soaked for at least four hours. Then, rinse and dry thoroughly. Drain and rinse the rice before cooking it.

Add 1 tbsp ghee and olive oil to a pan and boil. Black cumin (Shahi jeera), bay leaves, cinnamon, cardamom, cloves, and whole black pepper should be added. The onion should be added when the mixture starts to bubble. Add the paste of garlic and ginger now. Mix thoroughly. Season your recipe with a pinch of salt. Include a bit of water to ensure the spice doesn't burn when the cooking process is finished. Toss in the turmeric, red chili, cumin, and red pepper flakes. Toss in the mace-nutmeg paste. Continue cooking for another minute before removing from the heat.

Peas are now in the mix. Fry them for two minutes at a temperature of 350 degrees. From now on, add one cup of water at a time. Cover the pan and heat for approximately 5 mins or until the chicken is halfway cooked. Stirring is an ongoing process. The water should be drained entirely before adding rice and peas. Add 6 cups of boiling water, seal the lid, and cook on high heat.

*To avoid overheating:*
Stir often. Add the remaining ghee, green chilies, and fried onions once the water has evaporated and everything is cooked. After 10 minutes, remove the heat and cover the pot. Serve with Beef/Mutton Curry and Vuna Khichuri.

## CHINESE FRIED RICE RECIPE WITH SHRIMP

Servings:4
Prep:25-30 min Cook:30 min

**Ingredients**
- 1 cup of Chinigura/aromatic rice
- 200 gm Shrimp/boneless chicken
- 1/2 cup of Chopped cabbage
- 1/2 cup of Chopped carrot
- 1/2 cup of capsicum
- 1/2 cup of onion
- 4-5 pcs Chopped green chilies
- 2 tbsp Chopped green onion
- 1/4 tsp of every Ginger-garlic paste
- 2 tbsp Vegetable oil/butter
- 1/2 tsp Black pepper powder
- 1 tbsp Soy sauce
- 2 pcs Egg
- Salt

**Directions:**
Rinse rice thoroughly and allow it to soak for ten minutes before cooking. Water carries to a rolling boil in a large pot. Pour water over salt and one teaspoon of oil. To finish the meal, add the rice and simmer for around 90 % of its doneness. Drain and chill thoroughly. You may store the rice in the refrigerator for at least two hours before cooking. Using rice that was cooked the night before is also preferable. The butter or oil should be warmed in a pan. Add the paste of ginger and garlic and cook for a few seconds. Then, add the shrimp and the salt. Enable the food to cook for around two to three minutes.

Chicken can be substituted with shrimp. Then, add the vegetables, beginning with the toughest, including the green onion. A few minutes in the pan will do.

And meanwhile, keep the ingredients in the pan. Eggs and salt should be added. Eggs should be cooked to perfection. Toss thoroughly with the vegetables.

Add rice, black pepper, soy sauce, and salt to the mixture and combine thoroughly. Before adding salt, remember that soy sauce contains a small amount. You may include a little sugar in it if you like. For the next 2-3 minutes, keep stirring. After thoroughly cooking the rice, turn off the flame, and the ingredients are combined. Lemon juice and green onion should be slathered over and served at room temperature.

## NON-STICKY PULAO RECIPE

Servings:6
Prep:25-30 min Cook:45 min

**Ingredients**
- 3 cup ofs of Aromatic rice (Kalojeera/Chinigura)
- 1 tsp of every Ginger-garlic paste
- 2 tbsp Chopped onion
- one pc Bay leaf
- 3 pcs Cinnamon
- 4 pcs Cardamom
- 4/5 pcs Cloves
- 7/8 pcs Black pepper
- 1 cup of Hot liquid milk
- 5 cups of Hot water
- 1/2 cup of Vegetable/soybean oil
- 3 tbsp Ghee/clarified butter
- 4/5 pcs Green chilies
- Sugar
- Salt
- 8/10 pcs Raisin
- As required, Crispy fried onion/beresta

**Directions:**

For a ten-minute soak before cooking, thoroughly rinse the rice. Increase the heat to high and boil a large saucepan of water. Salt and one teaspoon of oil should be dissolved in water and salt. Toward the end of the dinner, add the rice and cook it until it's about 90% done. After draining and chilling sufficiently, you're ready to serve. Two hours before cooking, rice can be stored in the refrigerator. Even better: use rice that has already been cooked. The butter or oil should be melted in a pan. After adding the ginger and garlic pastes, cook for a few seconds. Afterward, add the shrimp and the salt. Two to three minutes of cooking time is recommended. The shrimp can be replaced with chicken. Add the green onion last when adding all the ingredients to the pot. There's no need to overcook it. Keep the elements in the pan simultaneously, and you'll be OK. There should be a few eggs and a little salt added. The ideal way to prepare eggs is to cook them just until they're set on the inside. Toss the vegetables with the sauce and serve.

*To taste:*
Stir in the rice, black pepper, soy sauce, and salt. Remember that soy sauce includes a little salt before adding any more salt. The sweetness level may be adjusted to your preference.

Keep stirring for the next two to three minutes. Once the rice is cooked and the ingredients are well combined, please remove it from the heat. Serve with lemon juice and chopped green onion.

## SPICY FRIED PUFFED RICE

Servings: 4
Prep: 10-15 min Cook: 15 min

**Ingredients**
- 2 cups of Puffed rice
- 1 tbsp Chopped onion
- 1/2 tsp Chopped garlic
- 2 tbsp Mustard oil
- 1/2 tsp Chopped ginger

- 1/4 tsp Turmeric powder
- 1 pcs Salt
- 1/2 tsp Chopped green chilies

**Directions:**
Heat oil in a frying pan. Mix in chopped onion, green chilies, and onion finely chopped garlic and ginger, turmeric powder, and salt. On medium heat, fry the food until it turns light brown. Mix in puffed rice and seasonings this time. Cook for 2–3 minutes at medium-low heat. Keep them away from the pan and turn off the heat. The ideal accompaniment is a cup of tea.

## MEAT RECIPES

# BEEF CURRY WITH POTATOES

**Ingredients**
- 1 kg Beef
- 1/2 cup of Vegetable oil
- 1/2 cup of chopped onion
- 1/2 tbsp Garlic paste
- 1/2 tbsp Ginger paste
- 2 tsp Dried red chili powder
- 2 pcs Bay leaves
- 3-4 pcs Cloves
- 1/2 tsp Coriander powder
- 1 tsp Cumin powder
- 1 tsp Turmeric powder
- 1/2 tsp Roasted cinnamon powder
- 1/2 tsp Roasted cardamom powder
- 1/2 tsp Roasted cumin powder
- two pcs Potatoes
- A pinch of turmeric or saffron powder
- 5-6 pcs Black pepper
- 2-3 pcs Cinnamon
- 3-4 pcs Cardamom

**Directions:**

Wash and drain the meat thoroughly before chopping it into little pieces. Rinse and drain the potatoes before adding salt and letting them sit for some time. Color can also be added using a sprinkle of turmeric or saffron powder. In a separate pan, heat enough oil for depth. Deep-fry the potatoes until they're browned. Set the potatoes aside after draining them off any excess oil.

Now, in a pan, heat the oil. Stir in chopped onions and cook until they're golden and transparent. Before adding the garlic and ginger paste, cook for a few minutes. A few drops of water are required to combine the spices. Cook until the spices begin to exude their oil. Then, add the meat chunks and stir them together well. Meat naturally produces water, so there is no need to add water. Cook for extra 5 mins, then remove from the heat.

Add water and cover the lid when the sauce becomes too thick. Cooking time should be at most 15 minutes. Include more water and simmer for 5 minutes if the meat is firm. Add the potatoes to the saucepan when the meat is almost done, cover with a lid, and simmer for 5 minutes. Add the turmeric powder once the water has been reduced by half and continue stirring until the meat exudes oil. Toss in a pinch of ground cardamom and cinnamon. Switch off the heat and sprinkle the toasted cumin powder over the mixture after another 2 minutes of stirring.

Here's your potato and meat curry, all set. Assemble the meal by heating the oil in a large skillet over medium-high heat.

# BANGLADESHI BEEF CHILI RECIPE

Servings:6
Prep:25-30 min Cook:30 min

**Ingredients**
- 300 gm Beef
- 1 cup of Broccoli
- 1/2 cup of Capsicum
- 1/2 cup of Onion
- 2/3 pcs Sliced green chilies
- 1 tbsp Soy sauce
- 1 tbsp Tomato sauce
- 2/3 pcs Dried red chili
- 1/2 tsp of every Ginger-garlic paste
- 1/2 tsp Sugar
- 2 pcs Tomato
- 1/2 tsp Black pepper
- 2 tbsp Vegetable
- 1 tsp Cornflour
- As needed Salt
- 1 tbsp Chopped green onion

**Directions:**
Slice the flesh into tiny, thin pieces. Make sure to wash and drain everything thoroughly. For roughly two hours, combine the ginger-garlic paste with half tsp soy sauce and a sprinkle of ground black pepper—time to prepare: Chop the vegetables into bite-sized pieces. Add water to the wash cycle and then drain. Heat the cooking oil in a pan before use. Add dried red chiles and cook until they turn a dark reddish-black. Continue cooking for 5-10 minutes or until meat is fork-tender. If necessary, you can add water. Toss in the vegetables and continue simmering for an additional five minutes. This time, include the leftover tomato sauce, soy sauce, black pepper, and sugar. Mix 2 tbsp of water and two tablespoons of cornflour in a bowl. Keep swirling as you slowly add this mixture. Serve with green onion on top when the sauce has thickened. Fried rice and beef chili are a delicious combination.

# DUCK CURRY WITH COCONUT MILK

Servings:6
Prep:15-30 min Cook:50 min

## Ingredients

- 1 kg Duck meat
- 1 cup of Coconut milk
- 1 tsp of every Ginger-garlic paste
- 1 tsp Cumin powder
- 1 tsp Coriander powder
- 1 tbsp Red chili powder
- 1 tsp Turmeric powder
- 1/2 cup of Chopped onion
- one pc Bay leaf
- 2 pcs Cloves
- 1/2 tsp Cinnamon powder
- 1/2 tsp Cardamom powder
- 3 tbsp Vegetable
- 1 tsp Roasted cumin powder
- As needed Salt
- 1/2 tsp Roasted cinnamon powder
- 1/2 tsp Roasted cardamom powder

## Directions:

Wash and drain the meat thoroughly before cutting it into little pieces. Now, in a pan, heat the oil. For a minute, add chopped onions, bay leaves, and cloves, and simmer until they're soft. There's no need to brown onions. Before adding the garlic and ginger pastes, cook the meal for a few more minutes. This is when to add cumin powder, red pepper, coriander powder, and a little water. Cook until the spices begin to exude their oil. Then, add the meat chunks and stir them together well. Meat naturally produces water, so there is no need to add water at this stage. Cook for extra 5 minutes, then remove from the heat. Adding water and closing the lid will help thicken and separate the oil from the spices. Cook, depending on the size of the casserole, for approximately 10 to 15 minutes. Include more water and simmer for 5 minutes if the meat is firm. Add turmeric powder and simmer for 2 to 3 minutes after the water has been reduced to half. Afterward, add 1 cup of coconut milk and water, if needed, and simmer for 15 to 20 minutes with the cover on. Add cardamom and cinnamon powder once the gravy has dried to your liking. Please take a look at it after another 5 minutes of cooking time. Sprinkle roasted spice powders, turn off the heat, and let it for two minutes. It's time to serve the dish with rice, naan, roti, chapatis, and other bread, such as pulao/pilaf.

## CHICKEN WITH CAULIFLOWER

Servings:6
Prep:15-20 min Cook:30 min

**Ingredients**
- one pc Cauliflower, medium size
- 800 gm Chicken
- 2 pcs Potato
- 1/2 cup of Chopped onion
- 1 tsp Ginger paste
- 1/2 tsp Garlic paste
- 1 tsp Cumin powder
- one pc Bay leaf
- 2 pcs Cinnamon
- 2 pcs Cardamom
- 1 tsp Turmeric powder
- 1 tsp Dried red chili powder
- 1 tsp Roasted spices powder
- 3 tbsp Vegetable oil
- Salt

**Directions:**
Cut the cauliflower and potatoes into bite-sized pieces first. Rinse well and drain. After that, shallow fried with a bit of oil. Set it aside for the time being. On a medium-high burner, heat the oil in a pan. Fry for a minute after adding the onion, bay leaves, cinnamon, and cardamom. Then, while stirring constantly, add the ginger-garlic paste, cumin powder, red chili powder, and salt. Then add the chicken and toss it around to combine it with the seasonings. Cook for 10 mins with the cover on, adding 1 cup of water if necessary. In about ten minutes, the bird will begin to discharge water. Potatoes and cauliflower should be added. Cook, covered, for 5-7 minutes. Stir occasionally to prevent

the sauce from scorching. When the water has nearly evaporated entirely, add the turmeric powder and stir until it begins to release oil. This time, add two and a half cups of water, or even more, depending on the thickness of the curry you desire this time. Cook on medium-high heat, covered, for another 15 minutes. When everything has been sufficiently cooked and the water has been decreased, turn off the heat. Serve with plain rice and a sprinkle of roasted spice powders while it's hot.

## HOMEMADE CHICKEN BUN RECIPE

Servings:7
Prep:1 hr Cook:45 min

**Ingredients**
*(Chicken Filling)*
- 500 gm Boneless minced chicken
- 1 tsp of every Ginger-garlic paste
- 1/2 tsp Black pepper powder
- 1 tsp Soy-sauce
- 2 tbsp Chopped onion
- 1 tsp Chopped green chilies
- 1 tsp Tomato sauce
- 1 tbsp Vegetable oil
- Salt

(Bun)
- 2 cups of Wheat flour
- 1 cup of Milk
- 2 tsp Yeast
- 1 tsp Sugar
- 1 tbsp Vegetable oil
- As needed Salt
- 1/3 cup of Beaten Egg
- As per requirement , Sesame seeds

**Directions:**
Set aside. Cook minced meat for 2-3 minutes. Add ginger-garlic paste, black pepper powder, salt, soy sauce, and water when the meat releases water. Cook until meat is tender. Cook for 2 minutes with

chopped green chilies, onion, and tomato sauce. Put it away. Take a warm milk cup. Mix in salt, sugar, and yeast. Ten minutes to activate the yeasts. Make a soft dough with it. Add some oil and keep it heated for 2 hours. The dough will double in size in 2 hours.

Spread some flour on a surface or table and knead enough dough for a few minutes. Then, load some dough with chicken mixture and form a bun. 7-10 minutes to swell. Then brush the bun with beaten egg and sprinkle with sesame or cumin seeds. Bake the bread for 25-30 minutes at 180°C in an electric oven. Baking the bread in a skillet takes 40-45 minutes at low heat. Your buns are ready.

## YOGURT AND CILANTRO MARINATED GRILLED CHICKEN

Prep: 20 minutes
Cook: 40 minutes
Servings: 2-4

**Ingredients**
- One chicken, cut into 6-8 pieces
- 2 cups of yogurt
- One large bunch of cilantro (coriander leaves) stems included
- 3 tsp of salt
- 1 1/2 tsp black pepper
- 2 tsp ground coriander
- 4-6 cloves of garlic
- 2-3 green chilies

**Steps**

In a blender, mix all ingredients into a paste. Marinate chicken in the paste for 1-2 hours. Drumsticks are made from thighs and bones. Chicken with Cilantro and Yogurt. Grill on high. To sear the chicken, place it on the hottest part of the grill. Grill for 5-10 minutes, depending on heat (you do not want the chicken to burn). Move the chicken to the cooler side using a gas grill or turn the heat down to medium-low.

Cook covered for 20-30 minutes.

# SPICY CHICKEN SPAGHETTI RECIPE

Servings:4
Prep:25-30 min Cook:20 min

**Ingredients**
- 250 gm Spaghetti
- 1/2 cup of Minced chicken
- 2 tbsp Butter
- 1 tsp Chopped garlic
- 1/2 tsp Chili flakes
- 2 tbsp Chopped capsicum
- Oregano-parsley
- 1/2 cup of Grated cheese
- 1/2 cup of Tomato sauce
- 1 tsp Soy sauce
- 1 tsp Oyster sauce
- 1 tsp Cooking oil
- As needed Salt
- To boil Water

**Directions:**
Bring some water to a boil. Boil salt, oil, and spaghetti. Cook, often stirring, over medium heat, until spaghetti is soft. The boiling time is 10-12 minutes. Rinse and drain properly.

Heat butter in a pan. Then brown chopped garlic and chili flakes. The soup is ready to serve. Fry for a while. Stir in minced chicken for 2–5 minutes until cooked. Stir in soy, oyster, and salt. Then tomato sauce. You may also use tomato puree—1 min.

Mix in the boiling spaghetti. Finish with oregano-parsley and grated cheese. Melt cheese and toss with spaghetti. Turn off the heat and serve warm. If desired, sprinkle with chopped coriander leaves.

# CHICKEN ROAST RECIPE

Servings:4
Prep:25-30 min Cook:30 min

**Ingredients**
- 1 kg whole chicken
- 1/2 cup of Vegetable oil
- 2 tbsp Ghee
- 1/2 cup of Chopped onion
- 2 tbsp Crispy fried onion
- 1 tsp Sugar
- 2 tbsp Powder Milk
- As needed Salt
- 2 pcs Bay leaves
- 1/2 tbsp Caraway/shah-jeera
- 6-7 pcs Raisin
- 3-4 pcs Prunes
- 1/2 cup of sour yogurt
- 1 and 1/2 tbsp Ginger-garlic pastes
- 3 tbsp Cashew nut paste
- 1 tbsp Dried red chili powder
- two sticks of cinnamon (long)
- 6 pcs Cardamom
- 5-6 pcs Cloves
- 1/2 tsp Black pepper
- 1/2 pc Nutmeg
- 2 pcs Mace
- 1/2 tsp White pepper

**Directions:**
Mix yogurt, ginger-garlic, cashew, and dried red chili powder in a small bowl. Mix with a spoon and beat into a paste. Put it away.
Mix dry spices/masala. Preheat the oven to 350°F. Grind all spices (except mace) in a bowl. Put it away.
Divide the chicken into four. Make holes with a knife so spices can readily enter during cooking. Drain well. Then dry the chicken with a kitchen tissue or a new towel. Now get a big bowl. Mix in salt and turmeric powder (optional).

Preheat 1/2 cup vegetable oil. Fry the chicken till golden. Remove from pan and set aside.1 tsp ghee in the remaining oil Stir in onion, bay leaves, and caraway (shah-jeera). Then add yogurt, dry seasoning mix, salt, and water. Stir for 2–3 minutes. Three minutes with fried chicken pieces and 1 cup water Cook covered for 10-15 minutes on medium heat. Add milk powder, sugar, dried prunes, and raisins when the gravy thickens. Cook for 2 minutes with the top off to let the oil out. Stop the heat. Add ghee and green chilies for more flavor. Serve with fried onions/barista. Warm pulao rice.

## CHICKEN CURRY RECIPE

Servings:6
Prep:15-20 min Cook:40 min

**Ingredients**
- 600 gm Chicken
- 4 pcs Potato, medium
- 2 tbsp Chopped onion
- 1 tbsp Garlic cloves
- 1 tbsp Chopped ginger
- 1 tsp Whole or crushed cumin
- 1 tsp Turmeric powder
- 6-7 pcs or as needed Dried red chili
- 3 pcs Cinnamon
- 3 pcs Cardamom
- 4-5 pcs Cloves
- 2 pcs Bay leaves
- 2 tbsp Soybean oil
- 1 tbsp Mustard oil
- Salt

**Directions:**
Preheat oven to 350°F. Drain Soybean & mustard oils (or any oils with increasing amounts) and salt. Hand-mix everything well. Switch on the heat, cover, and cook for 5 mins—no need to add water. Stir for a while, adding water if necessary to avoid burning. Cook covered for 5-7 minutes. Continue stirring for a few seconds longer before adding the water. Stir again, cover, and simmer until chicken and spices release oil. Add 2-3 cups of heated water to make

gravy. Cook covered on medium-high for 15-20 minutes. Stir to avoid scorching.

Meanwhile, taste and adjust the ingredients. When everything is cooked, and the gravy has reached the desired thickness, keep away from the heat and sprinkle with toasted cumin powder. Serve with rice, roti, naan, or paratha.

## HOMESTYLE CHICKEN KORMA

Prep: 30 minutes Cook: 45 minutes
Servings: 4

**Ingredients**
- 2 pounds bone-in chicken (dark meat best)
- two medium-peeled onions
- 1.5 inches chopped ginger
- four cloves garlic, chopped
- ½ cup of whole-milk yogurt
- 4 to 6 green cardamom pods
- 3 to 5 cloves
- two whole bay leaves
- one 3-in stick of cinnamon
- 2 tsp salt
- ½ tsp sugar
- 1 tsp black peppercorns
- 2 to 3 small hot green peppers
- 4 tbsp of ghee

**Steps**
Set aside one onion thinly sliced. The second onion, roughly chopped, is mixed with the garlic and ginger until smooth. If needed, add water. In a covered Dutch oven, cook the puree, chicken, yogurt, cardamom, cinnamon, peppercorns, and bay leaves for 10-15 minutes, stirring regularly. Bring to a low simmer. Cook until the achen is tender. Toss it now and 20–35 min. Stir in the chopped chilies and sugar. Add water or boil down the gravy to desired thickness. Brown the ghee and thinly sliced onions in a pan over medium heat. 5-7 min.
Salt the onions and add them to the korma.

# EASY BEEF TAHARI RECIPE

Servings:4
Prep:40 min Cook:1 hr 30 min

**Ingredients**
- 500 gm Aromatic rice (Basmati/Kalojeera)
- 700 gm Beef
- 1/2 cup of sour yogurt
- 1 tsp of every Ginger-garlic paste
- 1 tbsp Papaya paste
- 1/2 cup of Chopped onion
- 15 pcs Green chili
- 1/2 cup of Mustard oil
- 2 tbsp Ghee
- 2 tsp Sugar
- 8/10 pcs Raisin
- Salt

**Directions:**

First, make a spice mix or a special beef tahari masala combination. To create this, grind two big cinnamons, 7/8 black pepper, two tiny maces, two bay leaves, five kubeb (kabab chini), 7/8 white pepper, 1/2 tsp shah jeera, 6/8 cardamom, four cloves, 1/2 tsp jeera, 1/2 tsp coriander, and 1/2 nutmeg in a grinder. Put it away.

Wash the meat and drain well. Take tiny pieces in a basin. Mix the yogurt, ginger-garlic, papaya, spice/masala, and salt. 30 min marinade

Add chopped onion and green chilies to hot oil—1 min. Cook for 3-5 minutes with marinated beef. Not needed this time as the meat releases water. Cook until the water is gone. Then include 2 cups water and simmer until the meat is tender. 30-40 minutes max.

Remove beef from the pan when tender and the water has dried up. Now add rice and cook for 2-3 minutes. Then add hot boiling water and half as much rice. 3 tbsp powdered milk, mixed with water. Instead of powdered milk, use liquid milk.

Sugar and salt cook for 5 minutes on high heat, covered. Then mix in the cooked beef. Cook for 10 mins at low heat and cook on low heat for 10 minutes with the lid covered. Please turn off the burner and cover it with ghee. Cook covered for 10-15 minutes. Then your beef tahari is ready.

# MUTTON CURRY WITH POTATOES

**Ingredients**
- 1 kg Mutton
- 4 pcs Potato
- 1/2 cup of Chopped onion
- 1 tsp of every Ginger-garlic paste
- 1 tsp Cumin powder
- 1 tbsp Red chili powder
- 1/2 tsp Mace-nutmeg paate
- 1 tsp Papaya paste
- 1 tsp Turmeric powder
- As required, Roasted spices powder (Cinnamon, cardamom & cumin)
- 1/2 cup of Vegetable/soybean oil
- Salt
- 2 pcs Bay leaves
- 4 pcs Cloves
- 1/2 tsp every Cinnamon-cardamom powder

**Directions:**
Wash and drain the meat. Drain potatoes. Add salt and a pinch of turmeric or saffron powder for color. Preparing the oil Brown the potatoes in butter. Strain the potatoes and set aside. Continue cooking for a minute to soften the onions. Stir in garlic and ginger paste. Add cumin, red chile, cinnamon, cardamom, and water. Cook until the spices release oil. Add meat chunks and stir well. Add water is unnecessary because the meat is already moist—5 min. Add mace-nutmeg pastes and papaya paste when the spice mixture thickens and the oil separates. Cover with water and a lid. Cook for 20 min. Add more water and cook for 5 minutes if the meat is firm. Add turmeric powder and cook for 2–3 mins till the water is half.

Then add water to taste and simmer covered. Add the potatoes, shut the top, and simmer for 15–20 minutes. Turn off the fire and sprinkle the mix of roasted cardamom, cumin, and cinnamon powder. Serve warm with rice, roti, paratha, or naan.

# CATTLE HEAD VUNA

Servings:4
Prep:15-20 min Cook:30 min

**Ingredients**
- one pc Cow or goat head, large
- 1/3 cup of Chopped onion
- 1 tsp of every Ginger-garlic paste
- 1 tbsp Red chili powder
- 1 tsp Cumin powder
- 1 tsp Turmeric powder
- 3 pcs Cinnamon
- 4 pcs Cardamom
- 2 pcs Bay leaves
- 5-6 pcs Cloves
- 5-6 pcs Black pepper
- 1/2 cup of Soybean oil
- As needed Salt
- As required, Roasted cumin powder

**Directions:**
Cut the goat head into tiny pieces and remove any skin hairs. Then rinse and drain.
Place in a bowl. Salt, cumin, turmeric, red chili powder, and ginger-garlic pastes Hand-mix well and set aside for 30 minutes. In a pressure cooker, keep the heat medium-high. A saucepan can replace a pressure cooker. But it'll take a long time. Picky up the seasonings for a minute. The marinated headpieces CookCook for 3–5 minutes. Then add water to avoid spice burning and simmer covered until oil begins leaking. Stir constantly to avoid scorching. Then 3 cups hot water or as much gravy as you want. Close the cover and cook on medium heat for eight whistles or until the meat is done.
Meanwhile, taste the sauce and adjust seasonings like salt and chili powder. If the gravy is extra thin, simmer for 3-5 minutes more. Your curry will be ready now. Serve warm with plain rice, roti, naan, or paratha.

# STIR-FRIED BEEF

**Ingredients**
- 500 gm Beef/mutton tripe
- 1 pc Potato
- 1/3 cup of Chopped onion
- 1 tsp every Chopped ginger & garlic
- 4/5 pcs Dried red chili
- 3/4 pcs Cinnamon
- 3 pcs Cardamom
- one pc Bay leaf
- 3/4 pcs Cloves
- 1 tsp Cumin
- 1 tsp Turmeric powder
- 1/2 tsp Red chili powder
- 2 tbsp Vegetable oil
- Salt

**Directions:**
Wash the tripe well. Add salt, turmeric, and soybean oil, then chop it up. Add a tripe and a cup of water to a pressure cooker. 6 Whistles A saucepan with hot oil. Stir in bay leaf, cinnamon, cardamom, and cloves. Soak onion for a minute to remove the raw onion smell. Ginger, garlic, and cumin now. Stir everything thoroughly. Mix in the chopped potatoes.
Stir in the turmeric, red chili powder, and salt this time. Turn off the heat and serve warm over simple rice, roti, paratha, or naan.

# BEEF CABERNET

Prep: 20-30 minutes Cook: 1-1.5 hours
 Servings: 4-6
**Ingredients**
- 2 tbsp oil
- two ib beef, cubed to size 1/2 inch per side
- two medium shallots
- 1 or 2 fresh chilies
- 2 tsp of crushed garlic
- 2 tsp of crushed ginger
- 1 tbsp of cumin powder

- 1 tbsp of coriander powder
- 1/2 tsp turmeric
- 2 tsp of salt
- 1/2 tsp of black pepper
- 1 cup of a red wine
- 1/2 cup of milk
- one large carrot, cut into large chunks

**Steps**

Preheat oven to 200°C. In a medium saucepan, heat the oil. Add the cut shallots and stir fry until almost caramelized. Add the cubed meat and stir CookCook until the steak is browned. Stir sauté the ginger and garlic for 2-3 minutes. Stir sauté the turmeric, cumin, and coriander for 2-3 minutes. Pour in the wine, being sure to deglaze the pot. 4-5 minutes, occasionally stirring, cook for 4-5 minutes with milk—salt, pepper, and carrot pieces. Cover the pot and bake covered for 1–1.5 hours. Be cautious to check the lid every 1/2 hour to ensure the liquid hasn't evaporated altogether. If it's too dry, add 1/2 cup water.

## BEEF BRAIN BHUNA

Servings:4
Prep:15-20 min Cook:20 min

**Ingredients**
- 400 gm Beef/mutton brain
- 2 tbsp Chopped onion
- one pc Bay leaf
- 1/2 tsp Cinnamon powder
- 1/2 tsp Cardamom powder
- 1/2 tsp of every Ginger-garlic paste
- 1 tsp Dried red chili powder
- 1/2 tsp Turmeric powder
- 1/4 tsp Black pepper powder
- 1/2 tsp Cumin powder
- 3 tbsp Vegetable oil
- 3/4 pcs Green chilies
- Salt

**Directions:**
Clean the brain, including the veins, then chop it apart. Drain with lukewarm water. Please see the cleaning video below.
Mix spices/masala. Add cumin, red chile, cardamom, cinnamon, black pepper, salt, and water to a small bowl. Mix thoroughly with a spoon. Put it away. Set aside. Stir in onion, bay leaf, and cloves. Add ginger-garlic pastes and spices/masala mix, and simmer for 2-3 minutes. So the spices don't burn, add water. Cook for 2 minutes. Cook for 2-3 minutes with the brain. This time, add 1/2 cup water. Cook covered over medium heat. Cook 5-7 min. Stir often to prevent burning. Cook for a further 2 mins with the lid on, adding green chilies.

## CHICKEN NOODLE SOUP RECIPE

Servings:4
Prep:10-15 min Cook:20 min
**Ingredients**
- two packets of Noodles
- 1/2 tsp Ginger-garlic paste
- 1 tbsp Oil/ butter
- 1 tsp Chopped green chilies
- 1/2 cup of Boneless chicken
- 1/4 tsp Black pepper powder
- 1/2 tsp Red chili powder
- 2 tbsp Tomato sauce
- Vegetables
- Salt

**Directions:**
Cook in boiling oil/butter. Sauté ginger-garlic paste and green chilies for 30 seconds. Then include the chicken and cook for 2–3 minutes until cooked. Season to taste. If needed, add water. Cook for 2-3 minutes with the vegetables. Mix in the red chili powder. Then add water as needed. Add masala noodles. Please bring it to a boil—boiling water with noodles on medium heat. After a while, add tomato sauce and cook until the noodles are done. Turn off the heat and serve hot. Sprinkle with chopped green chilies.

## CHICKEN STEAK RECIPE WITHOUT OVEN

Servings:4
Prep:2 hour min Cook:20 min

**Ingredients**
- 4 pcs Boneless chicken breast
- 1/2 tsp of every Ginger-garlic paste
- 1/4 tsp Black pepper powder
- 1 tsp Soya sauce
- Just a pinch of salt
- 1/2 tsp Red chili powder
- 1 tbsp Butter

**Directions:**
Thinly slice chicken, Then rinse and drain—water saturating tissue paper. Add 2 tbsp liquid milk + 1 tsp lemon juice Mix thoroughly. Followed by a spice combination of red-haired chili powder-salt (Keep in mind salty soy sauce). Mix in the chicken with your hands. Then refrigerate in the refrigerator for at least 30 minutes, preferably longer.

Fry butter in a pan. Then cook on low heat until both sides are brown. It takes 10–15 minutes. Keep them away from the pan after they are well cooked on both sides. With ketchup or fried rice, serve.

## CHICKEN CHOW MEIN

Servings:2
Prep:15-20 min
Cook:15 min

**Ingredients**
- two packets of Noodles
- 100 gm Boneless chicken
- As required , Vegetables
- 1/4 tsp Chopped garlic
- 1 tsp Chopped green chilies
- 1 tbsp Soy sauce
- 1 tbsp Tomato ketchup
- 1 tsp Black pepper powder
- 2 tbsp Oil

- 1 tbsp Butter
- Sugar
- As needed Salt
- 1 tbsp Oyster sauce

**Directions:**
1 tsp cornflour, 1/2 tbsp soy sauce, black pepper, salt, red chili powder Mix thoroughly and set aside for 15 minutes.4 cups water (or enough to cook the noodles) and 1 tsp oil

Add the noodles when the water is thoroughly boiled and cook for 8 minutes. Never add noodles to cold or lukewarm water. Drain in a strainer, wash with cold water, then drain again. Brown the garlic and green chilies in the oil. Cook for 2–3 minutes with marinated chicken. Add hard vegetables, such as cauliflower, onions, and beans, and stir-fry over medium heat until half-cooked. Fry soft vegetables like cabbage, capsicum, beans, green peas, onion, etc. Add salt, keeping in mind the soy sauce salt afterward. Stir in soy sauce, tomato sauce, and pepper. Stir in boiling noodles, sugar (optional), and Ajinomoto/tasting salt (optional). Lastly, top with butter and spring onion (optional).

# BEVERAGE RECIPES

## PINEAPPLE JUICE RECIPE

Servings:2
Prep:10 min
**Ingredients**
- 2 cups Pineapple slice
- 2 tbsp Sugar
- 2 pcs Green chilies
- 1 tsp Black salt
- 3 cups of Water
- Ice

**Directions:**
In a blender jug, take a pineapple slice, black salt, green chili, water, sugar, and ice and blend very well.
Now strain the juice by a strainer and pour it into a glass. Your pineapple juice is ready to serve.

## GREEN MANGO JUICE

Servings:4
Prep:10-15 min Cook:10 min
**Ingredients**
- one pc Green mango
- 1 tsp salt
- 1/2 tsp Roasted cumin powder
- one pc Roasted red chili
- two pcs as needed Green chili
- 5/6 pcs Ice cube
- 2 tbsp Sugar
- 4 cups of Water

**Directions:**
Put everything in a blender jug—1 cup water. Then combine with 10-second pulses. Blend in ice cubes. Add 3 cups of water now. Blend thoroughly and serve mango juice.

# MILK TEA RECIPE

Servings:2
Prep:5 mins Cook:10 mins
**Ingredients**
- 1 Cup of Cow milk
- 1 tbsp Tea
- 1 tbsp or as need Sugar
- one pc Cardamom
- 2 pcs Cloves
- 2 pcs Cinnamon
- 2 pcs Black pepper
- 1 cup of Water
- two slices of ginger
- one pc Bay leaf

**Directions:**
Pour in the water and spices. Please bring it to a boil. Pour in the tea. 2–3 minutes boiling. Then add milk and boil. Then add sugar and mix well. Boil it for 5-7 minutes on low heat. Stir to avoid overflow. Turn off the flame when the color you want appears. Strain the tea and serve hot.

# SPECIAL SHARBAT RECIPE

Servings:2
Prep:30 mins Cook:10 mins
**Ingredients**
- sago
- 1/4 cup of Sugar
- 1/4 cup of Water
- 1/2 tsp Rosewater
- Food color
- 2 cups of Cold liquid milk
- Watermelon cubes

**Directions:**
Warm a big pan of water. Stir the sago grains in the water for 10-15 minutes. Add boiling water to half-cooked sago. Then add regular water and boil again. Turn off the heat when the sago becomes transparent. Drain the water and rinse the boiled sago. Drain and set

aside. Combine sugar, rose water, and red food color in another pan. Boil to a syrup. Put it away.

Mix sugar syrup, cooked sago, chilled milk, and diced watermelon in a big bowl. Serve with dry nuts and ice cubes.

## SWEET, SOUR, SPICY TEA

Servings:2
Prep:5 min Cook:10 min
**Ingredients**
- 1 tsp Tea
- As needed Sugar
- As needed Black salt
- 1 tbsp Tamarind pulp
- As required, Chopped coriander leaves
- As required, Chopped green chilies

**Directions:**
Prepare a kettle of water by bringing it to a boil. Boil 2–3 minutes with tea, sugar, salt, and tamarind. Strain and pour into teacups. Add green chiles, coriander, and lemon slices.
Hot serve.

## SWEET, SOUR TAMARIND JUICE

Servings 4
Prep 15 min
**Ingredients**
- 150 gm Tamarind
- Black salt
- Roasted cumin powder
- Red chili powder
- Sugar
- Salt
- Roasted coriander powder
- 4 cups of Water

**Directions:**
In a dish, combine 2 cups of water. Soak the tamarinds for 30 minutes in this water. Then, using your hand, take the pulp from the tamarinds and filter the tamarind juice water through a strainer. Add

another 2 cups of water and all of the juice's components, and thoroughly mix everything with a spoon. Then pour into a glass, place in the refrigerator, and serve cool.

## FISH CURRY WITH BEAN

Servings:6
Prep:15-20 min Cook:30 min
**Ingredients**
- 500 gm Bean
- 500 gm Fish
- 2 tbsp Chopped onion
- 5/7 pcs Sliced green chili
- 1 tsp Turmeric powder
- 1/2 tsp Mustard paste
- 2 pcs Tomato
- 2 tbsp Vegetable oil
- Salt
- 1 pc Potato

**Directions:**
Marinate the fish with salt and turmeric. After that, shallow fry in oil. Set it away.

Now, in a pan, heat the oil. Mix in the onion and green chilies. Fry for about a minute. Then add the beans, potato pieces, and salt and thoroughly combine everything. Cook with the lid on and some water. Add the mustard paste and turmeric powder when the water has been reduced for a few minutes. Cook for around 2-3 minutes. Add enough water to make the target quantity of gravy. This time, add the fish pieces. Cook, covered, on medium-high heat.

After a few minutes, add the tomato slices and cook for another 5-7 minutes. Your curry is done!

# FISH RECIPES

## FISH HEAD WITH MUNG DAL RECIPE

Servings:6
Prep:25-30 min Cook:40 min

**Ingredients**
- 1 cup of Mung Dal
- 1 pc Big fish head (Rohu/Katla)
- 2 pcs Bay leaves
- 5 pcs Cloves
- 5 pcs Black pepper
- 1/2 cup of Chopped onion
- 1 tbsp Ginger-garlic paste
- 1 tsp Cumin powder
- 1 tsp Red chili powder
- 1/4 tsp Cardamom powder
- 1/2 tsp Cinnamon powder
- 1/2 tsp Coriander powder
- 1 tsp Turmeric powder
- Salt
- 5-6 pcs Green chilies
- 1/2 cup oil
- 1/2 tsp Roasted cinnamon, cardamom & cumin powders

**Directions:**
Roast the mung dal over medium-high fire, stirring often. After that, it's 30 minutes of washing and soaking.
In a pan, heat the oil. Fry until the bay leaves, cloves, black pepper, and chopped onion are brown. Now stir in the ginger-garlic paste, cumin powder, cinnamon powder, cardamom powder, red chili powder, turmeric powder, coriander powder, salt, and a little water. Continue to stir for 3-4 mins. Then add the fish head pieces and thoroughly combine everything. Cover with the lid and add 1/2 cup of water—five minutes in the oven. Remove the fish headpieces from the pan and set aside. Cook for 5-6 minutes after adding the soaked dal. Then, include 1 cup of water, cover, and boil over medium heat for

approximately 30 mins. Then toss in the fish headpieces and give everything a thick sauce. The gravy can be thickened by adding as much water as required. Cook with the cover on medium-high heat. To avoid burning, keep stirring on a routine basis.

Add 5-6 green chilies and cover with a lid when almost done. Cook for an additional 2 minutes. Add roasted cinnamon, cardamom, and cumin powders, and turn off the heat. As well as rice or pulao, you may serve it with roti, paratha, or naan.

## RUI MACHER JHAAL KALIA – SPICY FISH KALIA

Prep: 30 mins Cook: 45 minutes
Servings: 4-6

**Ingredients**
- 2 lb fish, slice into 3/4 inch steaks
- 1 tsp cumin seeds
- one large bay leaf
- one large onion
- 3-4 garlic cloves
- 1/2 inch finely chopped ginger
- four green chilies slit down the middle
- 3 tbsp red chili powder
- 1 tsp cumin powder
- 1 tsp coriander powder
- 2 tsp sea salt
- 1/2 cup of cooking oil, preferably mustard oil
- 1/4 cup of yogurt
- 1 tsp sugar

**Steps**

Marinate the fish for 30 minutes with 1 tsp of turmeric and 1 tsp sea salt, then set aside. Bring a big pot of oil to a rolling boil over high heat. Once it's done frying, the fish should be golden brown. Remove the fish from the skillet. Heat on medium-low until the cumin seeds and bay leaf are spraying, then reduce the heat until the seeds are no longer spluttering and transfer to a separate pan. Stir in the onion, garlic, and green chilies until the onions caramelize for 3 to 4 minutes. Spices and 1/4 cup of water should be added; simmer over medium-low heat for about 5 minutes. Stir in the yogurt until it adheres to the pan, perhaps a minute or two more. Add the fish steaks and flip them over so that both sides are well-coated with the spices and seasonings. Then add 2 cups of water and carry it to a boil in a sizeable pan. Sprinkle in the remaining salt and the optional sugar if using (check for seasoning and add additional salt if necessary). The gravy should thicken in about 15 minutes, so lower the heat to medium-low and continue cooking for another 10 minutes.

## BHAPA CHINGRI –STEAMED SHRIMP WITH MUSTARD

**Ingredients**
- 1 lb medium/large shrimp
- 2 tsp brown mustard seeds
- 1 tbsp Water
- 1/4 cup of tbsp finely chopped onion
- two green chilies (Thai)
- 1/4 tsp ground turmeric
- 1/2 tsp red chili powder
- 3 tbsp mustard coil
- 1/2 cup of and an additional 1/4 tsp salt

**Steps**

1/4 cup of salt should be massaged into the shrimp before setting them aside for 5-10 minutes. Remove the salt by gently washing it with cold water and patting it dry. Transfer the mustard seeds to a stainless steel mixing bowl once coarsely ground. Add a tablespoon of water and thoroughly combine with the onion, green chili, turmeric, salt, chili powder, and oil in a large mixing bowl. Cover the bowl and set the shrimp aside for 10 minutes to marinate in the seasonings. Using a big pan (large enough to contain the stainless bowl), fill it with water until it comes up 1/3 up the bowl's sides. Bring to a rolling boil. Place the bowl in the pan and steam, covered, for about 8-9 mins or until the shrimp has turned translucent. Halfway through, give the shrimp a good stir.

## HILSA FISH FRY

Servings:3
Prep:15-20 min Cook:15 min
**Ingredients**
- 3 pcs Hilsa fish pieces
- 1/2 tsp Turmeric powder
- 1/2 tsp Dried red chili powder
- 1/2 tsp or as need Salt
- 1/4 cup of Chopped onion
- 2-3 pcs Sliced Green chili
- 1 tbsp Vegetable oil

**Directions:**
Remove the fish pieces from the water and place them on tissue paper to absorb excess moisture. Fish pieces should marinate in a large bowl covered with cooking spray or sprinkled with salt, turmeric powder, and chili powder for 5-10 minutes. The oil must be heated to medium-high heat in a frying pan, and the fish should be browned or crispy, depending on your preference. Onions and peppers should be added to the same oil and cooked for about 10 minutes or until the onions are browned. When the sauce is ready, serve the fish with plain, khichuri, or pulao rice.

## MASHED TILAPIA FISH

Servings:3
Prep:15-20 min Cook:15 min
**Ingredients**
- 5 pcs Tilapia fish
- 2 tbsp Chopped onion
- 1/2 tsp Finely Chopped garlic
- 4/5 pcs Dried red chilies
- 1/2 tbsp Mustard oil
- 2 tbsp Vegetable oil
- 1 tbsp Chopped coriander leaves
- 1/2 tsp Turmeric powder

- Salt

**Directions:**
For 30 minutes, marinate the fish pieces with salt and turmeric. Then lightly fried them in a frying pan with a bit of oil until they were golden brown. Fry some red chilies until they are dark brown in the same oil. Set it aside for the time being. Take a big mixing bowl. Mix in the fried red chilies, chopped onion, garlic, mustard oil, a pinch of salt, and the chopped coriander leaves until well combined. By hand, thoroughly mix all of the ingredients.

Remove the fish pieces from the bone and mash them with the mixture. The recipe is ready to be served when everything has been well combined and mixed. Serve with a side of plain rice.

## HILSA FISH IN MUSTARD SAUCE

Servings: 4
Prep: 30-35 min  Cook: 15 min
**Ingredients**
- 4 pcs Hilsa fish
- 3 tbsp Mustard oil
- 1 tbsp Mustard paste
- 1/2 cup of Chopped onion
- 5-6 pcs Green chili slice
- 2 tsp Turmeric powder
- Salt

**Directions:**
Wash and drain the fish. Now a bowl. Marinade the fish for 10 minutes with the seasonings.
Put the marinated fish in a pan. With 2 tbsp water and a lid, cook for 10 minutes on medium heat. So simple! Warm it up with rice.

# ROHU FISH KALIYA

Servings:10
Prep:10-12 min Cook:20 min

**Ingredients**
- 10 pcs Rohu fish
- 1/2 cup of Chopped onion
- 1 tbsp of every Ginger-garlic paste
- one pc Cinnamon
- one pc Cardamom
- 1 tbsp Cumin powder
- 1 tsp Coriander powder
- 1 tbsp Dried red chili powder
- 1tsp turmeric powder
- 1/3 cup of Vegetable oil
- 2 pcs Tomato
- 5/6 pcs Green chili
- Salt

**Directions:**

Salt and turmeric are the fish pieces. Fry both sides with a bit of oil. Put it away.

A saucepan with hot oil. Cinnamon, cardamom, and onion Cook for 2-3 minutes to remove the natural scent. Add the ginger-garlic paste, red chili powder, turmeric powder, cumin powder, coriander powder, and salt as desired. Mix thoroughly and heat for 2 minutes.

Now add tomato slices and water. Cover the pan and heat until the meat is tender and the sauce is oily. Bring two cups of boiled water. Add the fish. Cook covered for 10 minutes until the gravy thickens. Then add green chilies and cook for two minutes longer.

At this time, add some chopped coriander leaves. After 2 mins, turn off the heat and serve over plain rice or pulao.

## SPINACH WITH SHRIMP

**Ingredients**
- 600 gm Spinach
- 200 gm Shrimps
- 2 tbsp Chopped onion
- 4/5 pcs Green chilies
- 1 tsp Turmeric powder
- 2 tbsp Vegetable oil
- Salt

**Directions:**
Fry shrimp in some salt and turmeric in little oil and set aside. A pan of hot oil Sauté onions and green chilies. Then salt and spinaches. Add water and close the top. 5-6 min. The fried shrimp and turmeric powder Nicely combine. Then 1/2 cup water. Let it dry up. Serve with regular rice.

## OKRA WITH SHRIMP RECIPE

**Ingredients**
- 500 gm Okra, cut into 1."
- 1/2 cup of Shrimp, medium size
- 2 tbsp Chopped onions
- 5-7 pcs Green chilies
- 1/2 tsp Turmeric powder
- Salt
- 1 tsp Cumin powder
- 2 tbsp Vegetable oil

**Steps:**
Set aside. Onion and chili greens 1 min. Salt and turmeric powder to taste. Stir well and cook shrimp for 2-3 minutes.

Stir in the okra now. Cover with 1/2 cup water. 5-6 minutes on high heat. Add cumin powder and mix well after the water is half-dried. Include 1/2 cup water and simmer covered for 5-7 minutes.

Please turn off the heat after the water has dried up and the okra has released its oil.

# STEAMED HILSA FISH RECIPE

**Ingredients**
- 4 pcs Hilsa fish
- 1 cup of Chopped Onions
- 5/6 pcs Green chilies, sliced
- 1/3 cup of Mustard oil
- 1 tsp Mustard paste
- 1/2 tsp Turmeric powder
- Salt

**Directions:**
Drain fish pieces properly. A tissue absorbs excess water. Then mix 2 tbsp water and 2 tbsp mustard paste in an oven-proof basin. Mix thoroughly. Then mix in the fish.
Microwave the bowl for 5 minutes. After 5 minutes, delicately turn the fish using a spoon. Cook for 5 minutes more in the micro-oven. Keep the fish from the oven and check for medium rare. If not, cook for 2 minutes further and serve warm with rice.

**Tips:** Cooking time can be varied in different ovens.

# ROHU FISH VUNA RECIPE

Servings:6
Prep:15-20 min Cook:30 min

**Ingredients**
- 8 pcs Rohu fish
- 1 cup of Chopped onion
- 1 tsp of every Ginger-garlic paste
- 1 tsp Cumin powder
- 1 tsp Coriander powder
- 1/2 tsp Cinnamon-cardamom powder
- 1 tbsp Red chili powder
- 1 tsp Turmeric powder
- 1/2 cup of Oil
- 6-7 pcs Green chilies
- 1 pc Tomato

- Coriander leaves
- Salt
- 2 pcs Bay leaves

**Directions:**

Salt and turmeric are the fish pieces. Fry both sides with a bit of oil. Put it away.
Fry the onion and bay leaves in the remaining oil. Cook for 2-3 minutes till the raw scent fades away. Stir in a little water. Powders such as cinnamon and cardamom-cumin are now included. Cook until the oil separates. Cook covered for 2 minutes. Now add the fish and gently stir in the seasonings. One cup of water, a Spoon of fish, and heavy gravy require 10 minutes of boiling. Then add green chilies and cook for two minutes longer. Finally, add chopped coriander leaves. Turn off the heat and serve over simple rice or pulao.

## PARSHE FISH RECIPE

**Ingredients**
- 7/8 pcs Parshe fish
- one pc Potato, medium in size
- 1/2 cup of Chopped onion
- 6/7 pcs Green chili slices
- 2 pcs Tomato slices
- 1 tbsp Coriander leaves
- 2 tbsp Mustard oil
- 1 tsp Turmeric powder
- Salt

**Directions:**
Salt and turmeric powder fish pieces and shallow fried in oil. A pan Fish, potato, onion, green chile, turmeric, salt, oil, and tomato slices. Gently combine all ingredients.
Add 1 cup water and simmer on medium-high heat until the water is half dry. Stir gently while cooking to avoid scorching. After the water has been reduced to half its volume, add the chopped coriander leaves and 2-3 green chilies. Cook covered on low heat.
Serve with hot rice when you remove the dish from the heat.

## EASY HATE MAKHA ILISH RECIPE

Servings:6
Prep:10-15 min Cook:15 min
**Ingredients**
- 6 pcs Hilsa fish
- 1 cup of Chopped onion
- 5/6 pcs Green chilies
- 3 tbsp Mustard oil
- 1/2 tsp Turmeric powder
- Salt

**Directions:**
Wash and drain the fish. Now get a pan to cook. Add salt, mustard oil, and turmeric powder and mix them. Then mix in the fish pieces. Cover the pan with 1/2 cup water. Turn on the flame and cook for 10 mins or until the water has decreased. Warm it up with rice.

## BOTTLE GOURD RECIPE WITH SHRIMP

Servings:4
Prep:10-15 min Cook:20 min
**Ingredients**
- one medium-size Bottle of gourd
- 1/2 of a large size Potato
- 100 gm Prawn
- 2 tbsp Chopped onion
- 5/6 pcs Green chilies
- Salt
- 1/2 tsp Turmeric powder
- 1/2 tsp Cumin powder
- 2 tbsp Oil

**Directions:**
Cut gourd and potatoes. Fry shrimp in some salt and turmeric in little oil and set aside. Heat some oil in a pan. Sauté onions and green chilies. Add the gourd, potato, and salt. Add water and close the top. Cook for 2–3 minutes.

Then the turmeric, cumin, and fried shrimp. Nicely combine. Then add water to taste. Cook till the water is needed. Turn off the heat and serve with simple rice.

## HILSA FISH WITH BANANA

Servings:4
Prep:10 min Cook:25 min
**Ingredients**
- 500 gm Green banana
- 4 pcs Hilsa fish
- 2 tbsp Chopped onion
- 5/6 pcs Green chilies
- 2 tbsp Oil
- 1 tsp Turmeric powder
- Salt

**Directions:**
Wash bananas in turmeric powder. Drain well. Salt, turmeric powder, and oil shallow fried fish mix thoroughly. Put it away.
Set aside—onion and chilies 1-minute fry—next, bananas. Optionally add potatoes or jackfruit seeds. Stir in salt and turmeric powder. Boil water. Cook for 2 minutes when bananas are half-cooked and water dried.
Now add water to your curry's consistency. Cook, covered, for 5-7 minutes. Stir often. Remove the remove from heat and serve with rice.

## DELICIOUS FISH KEBAB RECIPE

Servings:6
Prep:20 min Cook:20 min
**Ingredients**
- 4 pcs Fish
- 150 gm Boiled, mashed potato
- 1 tbsp Fried onion
- 1 tsp Chopped green chilies
- 1 tbsp Chopped coriander leaves
- 1/2 tsp Cumin powder
- 1/2 tsp Coriander powder
- 1/2 tsp Garam masala powder

- 1/2 tsp Red chili powder
- 1 tsp Ginger-garlic paste
- Salt
- 1/2 Beaten egg
- Oil

**Directions:**
Salt and turmeric fried fish. Cool and gently remove the bones. Please put them in a big bowl.

All ingredients except oil are in a bowl. Now combine them thoroughly with your hands the fish. Then form into chops or cutlets. One egg in a small bowl. First, dip the cutlets in the eggs, then gently add the oil.

Patience is required to brown them on low heat. Remove them from the oil using a colander and place them on a tissue to absorb excess oil. Warm with ketchup or chutney.

## HILSA WITH SPINACH

Servings:4
Prep:20-25 min Cook:30 min

**Ingredients**
- one pc Hilsha fish head
- 500 gm Malabar spinach
- 2 tbsp Chopped onion
- 6/7 pcs Green chilies
- 2 tbsp Oil
- 1 tsp Turmeric powder
- Salt

**Directions:**
Heat vegetable and mustard oils. Onion and chilies 1-minute fry. Add water, turmeric, and salt. Cook for 2–3 minutes with fish headpieces. Remove just fish pieces. Set aside. Then add spinach to the sauce. Add salt, turmeric powder, and water. Cook a bit. Cook for 2 mins till the spinach is half-cooked and water dried.

Now add water to your desired sauce consistency. Cook for 5 minutes with the lid. Stir often. Keep away from the pan from the heat and serve with rice.

# EGGPLANT WITH PRAWN RECIPE

Servings:4
Prep:10-15 min Cook:30 min
**Ingredients**
- one pc Eggplant
- 8/10 pcs Prawns
- 2 tbsp Chopped onion
- 7 pcs green chilies
- one pc Potatoes
- 1 tsp mustard paste
- 1 tsp Turmeric powder
- 2 tbsp Oil
- Salt

**Directions:**
Salt, turmeric, and oil shallow fried fish mix all. Put it away. Cast aside. Onion and chilies 1-minute fry 3 cups water, salt, and turmeric powder. Boil it. Add eggplant and potatoes and cook covered for 5 minutes on medium-high heat. Then stir in mustard paste. Cook covered for 2 min.
Cook with the cover until the water is half gone. Tomato and two green chile slices provide flavor. Cook till done. Serve with rice.

# HILSA PILAF RICE RECIPE

Servings:5
Prep:20-25 min Cook:30 min
**Ingredients**
- 5 pcs Hilsa fish
- 1 tsp of every Ginger-garlic paste
- 1/3 cup of Chopped onion
- 8-10 pcs Green chilies
- 1/2 tsp Red chili powder
- 1/2 cup of sour yogurt
- 3 pcs Cinnamon
- 2 pcs Cardamom
- one pc Bay leaf
- Salt
- 1 tsp as need Sugar

- 1/2 cup of Vegetable oil
- 1 tbsp Ghee
- Crispy fried onion

**Directions:**

Cut hilsa fish. Drain well. Soak extra water in tissue paper.
Preparing the oil, Chop onion and green chilies. Fry until tender. Continue cooking for 2–3 minutes until the oil comes from the ginger-garlic paste. Then add fish and cover. Continue cooking the fish for a further 2 minutes after gently turning it. Add water and cooked onion now. Cook for 5 minutes more. Then carefully remove the fish, leaving the spices behind. Aside from that, Stir in cinnamon, cardamom, and bay leaf, then pre-washed and drain the rice. Keep stirring for 2–3 minutes until the rice pops. Then 6 cups of water. Sugar and salt Cook covered on medium heat. When the rice is dry, add the fish pieces. 1 tbsp ghee and crispy fried onions
On low heat, cover and simmer for another five minutes. Cover the flame and put it out after five minutes. Carefully pull the rice up and down to remove the fish chunks. Serve hot hilsa pilaf with salad.

## BANGLADESHI SMALL FISH RECIPE

**Ingredients**
- 200 gm Mourala/Mola Fish
- 2 pcs Potato
- 1/2 cup of Chopped onion
- 6/7 pcs Green chili slices
- 2 pcs Tomato slices
- 2 tbsp Vegetable oil
- 1 tbsp Mustard oil
- 1 tbsp Coriander leaves
- Salt
- 1 tsp Turmeric powder

**Directions:**
Take a pan. Combine the fish, potato, onion, green chili, turmeric powder, salt, oils, and tomato in a large mixing bowl. Gently combine everything with your hand.

Add 1/2 cup water, increase the heat to medium-high, and cook up to the water has evaporated to half its original volume. To avoid burning, slowly and carefully stir a few times during cooking.
Season with chopped coriander leaves and 2-3 green chilies once the water has been reduced to half. Cook over medium-low heat, covered.
Allow to cool completely before serving over rice. Remove from heat once all the water has evaporated, and all the oil has separated, and serve immediately.

## HILSA FISH WITH ARUM

Servings:4
Prep:20-25 min Cook:30 min
**Ingredients**
- 4 pcs Hilsa fish
- 1 kg Arum
- 8/10 pcs Green chilies
- 2 tbsp Chopped onion
- 1/4 cup of Oil
- 1/2 tsp Turmeric powder
- Salt

**Directions:**
Arum should be cut into pieces and cleaned. Bring salt to a boil for 2–3 minutes and drain well. Slightly fried fish in a shallow fryer with salt, turmeric powder, and oil. It should be set aside.
In a pan, heat the oil. Combine the onion and green chilies. Cook for one minute. After that, add the cooked arum. Stir in the salt and turmeric powder for a few seconds. Bring water to a boil. Cook for 2 mins or up to the potatoes are halfway cooked, and the water has been absorbed entirely.
Now add water until the curry reaches the desired consistency. Cook, covered, for 5-10 minutes. Occasionally, stir. When thoroughly cooked, keep away from the heat and serve with rice.

# ROHU FISH WITH EGGPLANT

Servings:6
Prep:10-15 min Cook:20 min
**Ingredients**
- 500 gm Eggplant/aubergine
- 5/6 pcs Rohu fish
- 2 tbsp Chopped onion
- 5-7 pcs Green chilies
- 1 tsp Turmeric powder
- 1 tsp Mustard paste
- 2 pcs Tomato
- 2 tbsp Vegetable oil
- As needed Salt

**Directions:**
Mix salt, turmeric powder, and oil shallow fried fish. Place aside. In a pan, heat the oil. Combine the onion and green chilies. Cook for one minute. After that, add 3 cups of water, salt, and turmeric powder. Turn the heat to high and carry it to a boil. While the water is boiling, add tiny slices of eggplant and simmer, covered, for 5 minutes over a medium-high temperature. Then add the mustard paste and combine thoroughly. Cook, covered, for 2 minutes. Add the fish pieces and simmer, covered, until the water is reduced to half. To add flavor, add tomato slices and two green chilies. Cook until thoroughly cooked. Serve with rice after taking it out of the oven.

# HOMEMADE FISH FINGER RECIPE

Servings:4
Prep:45 min Cook:15 min
**Ingredients**
- 300 gm Boneless fish
- 1/2 tsp of every Ginger-garlic paste
- 1 tsp Soy sauce
- 1 tsp Red chili powder
- Just a pinch of Black pepper
- 1/2 tsp Lemon juice
- 1 pcs Egg
- 1/4 cup of Wheat flour

- 1/2 cup of Breadcrumb
- Oil
- Salt

**Directions:**
Consider any boneless fish. Cut into 3 cm length by 1 cm broad pieces. Then thoroughly wash and drain. The tissue paper may be used to absorb excess water. Now marinate fish pieces for 30 minutes using a ginger-garlic paste, black pepper, red chili powder, soy sauce, lemon juice, and salt (be careful of the salty soy sauce).

After 30 minutes: Sprinkle flour over the fish pieces. Dip it in a beaten egg.

Following that, sprinkle with breadcrumbs. This procedure should be repeated for all parts. Refrigerate them for 10 minutes to set. Remove from the refrigerator and deep fry on medium-low heat until they are dark brown.

Serve with ketchup or fried rice of your choice.

## SPICY FISH FRY

**Ingredients**
- one pc Any boneless fish like tilapia, coral (Whole, 250 gm)
- 1/2 tsp Garlic paste
- 1/2 tsp Ginger paste
- one pinch of Black pepper powder
- 1 tsp Soya sauce
- 1/2 tsp Dried red chili powder
- 1/2 tsp Lemon juice
- 1 tsp Cornflour
- 1/3 cup of Vegetable oil to fry
- Salt

**Directions:**
Properly wash and drain the fish, and wipe excess water from the fish using tissue paper. Using a sharp knife, make vertical cut marks on both parts of the fish to allow the spice mix to penetrate the flesh during marinating.

Now, combine all ingredients except the oil and create a paste. Mix this mixture over both sides of the fish as much as possible with your hands or a brush and place in the refrigerator for half an hour to marinate.

Fry the fish on all sides for 10-15 minutes in a frying pan heated to medium heat. When the fish seems charred in color, it is time to serve the Masala Fish Fry.

## MAWA GHAT ILISH LEJ VORTA

Servings:4
Prep:10-15 min Cook:20 min

**Ingredients**
- 4 pcs Hilsa tail
- 4/5 pcs Dried red chilies
- 2 pcs Chopped green chilies
- 1/4 cup of Chopped onion
- 3 tbsp Mustard oil
- Salt

**Directions:**

Properly wash and drain the fish pieces. Season with salt and turmeric. Fry both sides on medium heat. Keep away from the oil. In the same oil, fry some dried red chilies.

Allow to cool somewhat before deboning the fish pieces. They should be placed in a mixing bowl. Combine onion, fried chilies, green chilies, salt, and mustard oil in a food processor. Now combine everything with the fish and mix thoroughly. Serve immediately over plain rice, khichuri rice, or pulao rice.

# VEGETABLE RECIPES

## VEGETABLE EGG NOODLES RECIPE

**Ingredients**
- 250 gm Stick noodles
- 2 pcs Egg
- 1/2 cup of Chopped carrot
- 1/2 cup of Chopped cauliflower
- 1/2 cup of Chopped cabbage
- 1/3 cup of Chopped bean
- 1/3 cup of Chopped onion
- 2-3 pcs Sliced or chopped green chilies
- 1 tsp minced garlic
- 3 tbsp Vegetable oil
- 1/2 tsp Crushed black pepper
- 1 tsp tasting salt
- 1 tbsp Soy sauce
- Salt
- 1 tsp Sugar

**Directions:**
Boil water in a pan with 4 cups or enough water to cover the noodles and one teaspoon of oil. When the water starts to boil, include the noodles and continue cooking until they reach an internal temperature of 80%. Never add noodles to cold or lukewarm water. Drain in a strainer, rinse with cold water, then drain again.

2 tbsp oil in a small pan. Add the beaten eggs and salt and scramble them with a spatula. Fry until well cooked. Please remove them and set them away. Bring another 1 tbsp of oil to a boil in the same pan. Add the hard vegetables, such as cauliflower and carrots, and sauté on moderate to medium-high heat, often tossing, until half-cooked.

Add soft vegetables such as cabbage, capsicum, beans, and green peas, and cook for 2-3 mins. Season with salt, considering the salt in the soy sauce that will be added later.

Stir in the green chile and onion and, after a few minutes, the crushed black pepper or powder. Stir in the boiling noodles, scrambled egg, sugar (optional), Ajinomoto/tasting salt (optional), and soy sauce until thoroughly combined. Finally, scatter some spring onion on top (optional). Serve immediately.

## STIR-FRIED CABBAGE WITH GARLIC AND BENGALI SPICES

Prep: 10 minutes Cook: 30 minutes
Servings: 4-6

**Ingredients**
- 1/2 head of cabbage shredded thinly
- 2 tbsp ghee
- 1-2 dried red chili
- 4-6 cloves garlic, chopped
- 1/2 tsp black mustard seeds
- 1/2 tsp nigella
- 1/2 tsp cumin seeds
- 1 tsp of salt
- Fresh back pepper

**Steps**

Using a wok or big pan, heat the ghee over medium heat. Stir in the dry chili and three spices until the spices begin to crackle. Add the fresh garlic and cook until the garlic becomes a rich golden color and seems nearly caramelized. Stir in the cabbage up to it is coated with the ghee and spices. Add the salt and mix until the cabbage is uniformly covered once more. Continue stirring for extra 5 mins or until the cabbage has wilted. Turn the flame to low heat and cook covered for 10-15 mins, stirring periodically. Just before serving, sprinkle with crushed pepper.

# DHAROSH BHAJI (OKRA)

Prep: 20 minutes. Cook: 15-20 minutes
Servings: 4

**Ingredients**
- 2 pounds of fresh okra cut into quarter-inch slices
- 1/2 a medium onion
- two cloves of garlic
- 1 tbsp of cooking oil
- 1 tsp of salt
- 1/4 tsp of pepper
- 1/2 tsp cumin
- 1/2 tsp red turmeric
- 1/2 tsp red chili powder (optional)

**Steps**

Heat oil in a frying pan, preferably nonstick, over medium-high heat. When the oil is heated, include the onion and garlic. Stir and cook up to the garlic begins to caramelize. Stir in all the spices for a minute. Add the okra and toss until it is well covered with the spices. Reduce to medium heat and cook, stirring periodically, uncovered. Your personal preference will determine your doneness. My favorite is to continue cooking until the okra becomes caramelized as well.

# PALONG SHAAK BHAJI – SPINACH BHAJI

**Ingredients**
- 1 pound chopped spinach
- 1 tsp salt
- 1 tsp panch phoron
- 1/4 tsp black pepper
- 1-2 dried red chilis
- 1/4 cup of onions
- 1-2 cloves garlic, finely chopped
- 1 tbsp cooking oil

**Steps**

In a medium-high-heat pan, heat the oil. Fry an extra 1 minute before adding the dried red chilis. Cook until the onions are translucent. Stir-fry the garlic and paanh phoron until the spices begin to sputter. Combine the spinach, salt, and pepper in a large bowl, stirring well to cover the leaves with the spices. Cook for 15-20 minutes, or until the spinach is thoroughly wilted and protected, over medium heat.

## CHICHINGA BHAJI – FRIED ZUCHHINI

Prep: 15 minutes Cook: 30 minutes
Servings: 4

**Ingredients**
- 1 tbsp oil
- 1/2 tsp kalojira
- 1 tsp cumin seeds
- 1 or 2 dried red chili
- one large onion, chopped
- 1 or 2 cloves of garlic
- three medium zucchini, peeled and cubed
- 1 tsp coriander powder
- 1 tsp cumin powder
- 1/4 tsp red chili powder
- one medium bay leaf
- 1/4 cup of yogurt

**Steps**

In a saucepan, carry the oil to a boil over medium heat. Fry for 1 minute before adding the nigella and cumin seeds. Fry the onion and garlic until transparent. Add the zucchini and the remaining ingredients to the pan and raise the flame to high (excluding the yogurt). Stir fry for 5 minutes, then lower to a medium setting. Cook, covered, occasionally stirring, until the zucchini is tender (15-20 minutes). Stir in the yogurt and cook for 5 minutes more.

# VEGETABLE PULAO

**Ingredients**
- 2 cups of rice
- 1 cup of mixed vegetables, diced
- 2 tbsp ghee
- 1 tbsp ginger paste or powder
- one bay leaf
- 1/2 cup of chopped onions
- 1 tsp chopped garlic
- 1/2 inch ginger grated
- 4 cups of water
- 3 tsp salt

**Steps**

In a saucepan on medium flame, heat the ghee. Reduce the heat to low and sauté the onions and garlic until transparent. Sauté for about a minute before adding the ginger paste/powder and bay leaf. Add the rice and sauté for 3-5 mins, or up to the rice is completely covered in ghee. Incorporate the water and salt (or the stock). Bring to a rolling boil. Reduce heat to a simmer. Cover and cook on low heat for 23 minutes.

# BEGUN BHAJI (FRIED EGGPLANT)

Prep: 10 minutes Cook: 30 minutes
Servings: 2-4

**Ingredients**
- One large eggplant sliced 1/4 inch thick
- 1 tsp turmeric powder
- 1 tsp cumin powder
- 1/2 tsp cayenne chili powder
- 1/2 tsp garlic powder
- 1 tsp salt
- 1/4 tsp garam masala
- 3 tbsp olive or mustard oil.
- Additional oil for frying

**Steps**

Combine all spices and oil in a bowl and mix. Cover the sliced eggplant on both sides and put aside. Heat a single layer of oil on high heat in a frying pan. When the oil begins to smoke, add one layer of eggplant to the pan (as much as possible). Keep the heat low to medium-low and continue to saute onions until the vegetables are almost done but not burned. Cook the opposite side as well. You may need to include more oil and increase the heat.

Continue cooking the slices in this manner until all of them are done.

## LAU BHAJI – BOTTLEGOURD BHAJI

Prep: 15 minutes Cook: 15 minutes
Servings: 2-4

**Ingredients**
- 1 medium lau
- 2 tsp whole cumin seeds
- two green chilies, slit into halves lengthwise
- 1 inch finely chopped
- fresh ginger
- one clove of finely chopped garlic
- 1/2 teaspoon turmeric powder
- 1/2 teaspoon coriander powder
- 1 tbsp oil
- 1/4 cilantro finely chopped
- salt

**Steps**

Peel and then thinly slice the gourd. In a frying pan, heat the oil. Simmer the cumin seeds and chilies in the hot grease until the seeds start to spatter. Stir in the ginger for a minute or two. Stir in the gourd and cook, covered, over medium heat for approximately 5 minutes. Combine turmeric powder, coriander powder, salt, and 1/4 cup water. Continuing to cook for extra 5 mins, or until the gourd is mushy and the skin has softened, is recommended. If preferred, garnish with a sprinkling of chopped cilantro before serving.

# SPECIAL MIX VEG RECIPE

Servings:4
Prep:15-20 min Cook:20 min

**Ingredients**

- 500 gm Seasonal mixed vegetables
- 1 tsp Special spices mix
- 2 pcs Bay leaves
- 2 pcs Cardamom
- 3 pcs Cinnamon
- 3 pcs Green chili
- 4 pcs Dried red chili
- 1/2 tsp Cumin powder
- 1/2 tsp Turmeric powder
- 1/2 tsp Ginger paste
- 1 tsp Sugar
- 1/2 tbsp Cornflower
- 3 tbsp Vegetable oil
- As needed Salt

**Directions:**

This recipe is adaptable to any seasonal vegetables. I used potato, aubergine, pointed gourd, and pumpkin. Vegetables should be cut into tiny pieces and well-washed and dried.

In a pan over medium-low heat, heat some oil. Fry bay leaves, cinnamon, cardamom, dried red chilies, green chilies, and a mixture of spices called "Panch foron" till brown. However, avoid overcooking the curry; else, it will taste harsh. After that, add the vegetables and salt. Combine and cook, covered, for 5-7 minutes. There is no requirement to add water at this step—the water emitted by vegetables aids the cooking process. Combine cumin powder, turmeric powder, and ginger paste in a mixing bowl. Stir for a minute to eliminate the raw spice scent. Then include 3 cups of water and cover the container with the top. Cook over medium-high heat. Add

sugar to taste after some water has reduced and the vegetables are cooked.
In a bowl, combine cornflower and regular water. Then gently incorporate this into the curry to thicken it. Continue stirring as you add the cornflour. Cook for a further minute, and your curry is ready to serve with luchi (Bhature/deep-fried bread) or paratha.

## CHICKEN CURRY WITH POTATO

Servings:5
Prep:15-20 min Cook:30 min

**Ingredients**
- 500 gm Chicken
- 2 pcs Potato (Medium in size)
- 1/2 cup of Chopped onion
- 1 tsp of every Ginger-garlic paste
- 1 tsp Cumin powder
- 1tsp Dried red chili powder
- 1 tsp Turmeric powder
- 2 pcs Bay leaves
- 2 pcs Cloves
- 2-3 pcs Cinnamon
- 3-4 pcs Cardamom
- 1/2 tsp Roasted cardamom powder
- 1/2 tsp Roasted cinnamon powder
- 1/2 tsp Roasted cumin powder
- 1/4 cup of Vegetable oil
- Salt

**Directions:**
Chicken and potatoes should be cut into tiny pieces. Thoroughly clean and drain. Now, in a saucepan, heat some vegetable oil. For two minutes, stir in the chopped onions, bay leaves, cinnamon, cardamom, and cloves to eliminate the raw onion scent. Add the ginger-garlic paste, cumin powder, red chili powder, and salt at this stage. Combine and mix everything well for a few minutes. This time, include chicken and potatoes. Provide a nice mixture. Preheat

oven to 350°F. Stir in the chicken after about 15 mins, or up to the chicken is cooked thoroughly and the liquids clear.

This time, add the turmeric powder and cook until the curry begins to release oil. Then include 2 cups of water and cook for 10-15 minutes. Combine roasted cinnamon and cardamom powder in a mixing bowl for 2 minutes. Turn off the fire and sprinkle the top with toasted cumin powder; the dish is ready to serve. This chicken curry goes well with rice, roti, naan, or paratha.

## POTATO STUFFED PARATHA RECIPE

Servings:4
Prep:30-35 min Cook:20 min

**Ingredients**
- 1 and 1/2 cups Wheat flour
- 1 cup of Boiled potato
- 1 tsp Chopped onion
- 1 tsp Chopped green chilies
- one pc Roasted/fried dried chili
- 1 tbsp Chopped coriander leaves
- 1/2 tsp Roasted cumin powder
- 1/2 tbsp Roasted coriander powder
- 1/2 tsp Chat masala powder
- Ghee/oil
- Salt

**Directions:**
Combine flour, salt, and 1 tbsp oil in a bowl. With your hand, gently combine them. Slowly and steadily add water until a soft dough develops. For 2-3 minutes, knead the dough until smooth. After the dough has been greased and covered, it should rest for 30 minutes.

In the meantime, prepare the potato for staffing. Combine mashed potatoes, green chilies, onion, dried chile, coriander leaves, cumin powder, coriander powder, chat masala, and salt in a large mixing bowl. It should be set aside.

Now divide the dough into five equal pieces. Take out all amount and form it into a ball by hand. To create a room within a ball, flatten it using your hands. Fill the center with potato filling and seal it by extending the borders toward the center. Using a roller, flatten the dough to the same thickness as the paratha we prepare at home or slightly thicker.

Preheat a pan and add a paratha. For one minute, heat. Then flip it over and continue heating for an additional minute. Spread oil, butter, or ghee on both sides and cook till golden. Then carry it out of the oven and serve it immediately, if possible.

## POTATO CHOP RECIPE

Servings:6
Prep:25-30 min Cook:30 min

**Ingredients**
*(For batter)*
- 1 and 1/2 cups of Gram flour
- 3 tbsp Rice flour
- 1 tbsp Cornflour
- 1 tsp Ginger-garlic paste
- 1/2 tsp Roasted cumin powder
- 1 tsp Roasted coriander powder
- 1 tsp Red chili powder
- Salt

*(For potato cutlet)*
- 4 pcs Boiled potatoes
- 1 tsp Fried onion/beresta
- 6/7 pcs Roasted & crushed red chili
- 1 tsp Chopped green chili
- 1 tsp Roasted & crushed cumin-coriander
- As needed Salt
- To deep-fry Oil

**Directions:**
To start, we'll prepare the batter. Add the gram flour, rice flour, cornflour, ginger-garlic paste, roasted cumin powder, red chili powder, roasted coriander powder, and salt to a sizeable bowl and mix well. Mix well. With a spoon, combine all dry ingredients. Then,

adding normal-temperature water gradually creates a smooth batter. The batter must be thick enough and thick enough. It must be placed aside for the time being.

Now, in a separate mixing bowl, place the mashed potatoes that have been cooked. Combine the fried onion, roasted red chile, chopped green chili, cumin, coriander, and salt in a large mixing bowl. Then cut into small shapes such as chop or potato cutlets, or as you choose. This will keep for around 20 to 30 days in a plastic box in the refrigerator. At this time, heat the cooking oil in a deep-fryer pan. While the oil is still slightly hot, dip the all potato cutlet into the batter and coat it with the batter. Then With a fork, insert it into the heated oil. On low, medium heat, cook one side till brown.

If you want the second side to be as brown as the first, fry it for another 5 minutes.

Once both sides are finished, remove them from the oil and put all of them on a tissue to absorb any extra oil. Now continue serving your favorite foods. Sprinkle some rock salt on top to enhance the flavor.

## POTATO PAKORA RECIPE

Servings:4
Prep:15-20 min Cook:20 min

**Ingredients**
- 1 cup of Finely chopped potato
- 2 tbsp Chopped onion
- 1 tsp Chopped green chili
- 1/2 tsp Ginger paste
- 1/4 tsp Roasted cumin powder
- 1/4 tsp Roasted coriander powder
- 1 tsp Chopped coriander leaves
- Three tsp+1 tsp Gram flour
- Salt

**Directions:**
Mix everything that isn't oiled except for the oil into a bowl. Add a few drops of water. Now, using your hand, combine. To make a good batter, it should not be too wet. It should be a little dry, though.

To deep fry, heat oil in a pan over medium heat. Take some batter, form it into pakoras, or cut it up as you wish. Patience is required while frying steadily over medium-low heat until brown. When finished, squeeze them from the oil and place them on tissue paper to absorb the leftover oil. Serve warm with the ketchup or chutney of your choice.

## LONG BEAN RECIPE
Servings:4
Prep:20 min Cook:20 min
**Ingredients**
- 250 gm Long beans
- 100 gm Shrimps
- 2 tbsp Chopped onion
- 7-8 pcs Green chilies
- 5-6 pcs Garlic
- 1/4 tsp Cumin
- 1 tbsp Mustard oil
- 1 tbsp Cooking oil
- Salt

**Directions:**
In a pan, heat the oil. Fry the prawns/shrimp in a stove pan with salt and turmeric powder, then serve them. Add the garlic, green chilies, and cumin when golden brown, cook for another minute or two, then serve. Add the pre-boiled long beans and salt to the pan and cook on keep the medium flame for 2-3 mins. Please turn off the heat and let the fire cool down so they don't burn.

Now, using a blender, blend the mixture into a smooth paste. You may do this with a traditional sheel-pata (indigenous grinder). Add onion, green chilies, and mustard oil now. With your hands or a spoon, combine all of the ingredients. Borboti Chingri Vorta is now available for service. Accompany with plain rice.

# CHINESE VEGETABLE RECIPE

Servings:4
Prep:10-15 min Cook:30 min

**Ingredients**
- 500 gm Vegetables (Broccoli. Chinese cabbage & bok choy)
- 1/2 tsp Chopped garlic
- 2/3 pcs Dried red chili
- 3/4 pcs Chopped green chilies
- 1/2 cup of Chopped onion
- 2 tbsp Oil
- 1/2 tsp Black pepper powder
- Salt
- 2 tbsp Cornflour
- Sugar

**Directions:**

Heat the needed water with a grain of salt in a pan over high heat and bring it to a boil. Salt aids in the preservation of the hues of vegetables. Add vegetables and bring to a boil for 1 minute. Drain the water, but save the vegetable stock for future use.

Combine 1/2 tsp dark soya sauce, 1/2 tsp oyster sauce, and 1 tsp tomato ketchup to make a sauce. Include some water to get the desired consistency. It should be set aside.

Put the oil on the stove over high heat in a large skillet and let it warm. Chopped Garlic and red chilies are fried in a pan until golden brown. You may replace marinated chicken/prawns if desired. Then add the boiling veggies and continue stirring for a few minutes. For a bit, add the onion and green chilies. Now stir in the sauce mixture, salt, and pepper powder. Stir well to combine everything. Add 1 & 1/2 cups of or as needed of previously-stored vegetable stock. Cook for approximately 6-7 minutes until the desired gravy consistency is achieved.

Taste and adjust spices as needed after the vegetables are tender, then add sugar. Combine 2 tbsp cornflour and 2 tbsp of normal water in a bowl. Add this combination to the vegetables and stir thoroughly to avoid corn flour balling. After adding the cornflour mixture, the sauce becomes thick. For another minute, cook the food. Then include the lemon juice and mix it in. Your Chinese Vegetable is now complete. Alternatively, put chopped spring onions on top. Serve immediately with Chinese fried rice.

## PAPAYA WITH MUNG DAL

Servings:4
Prep:10-15 min Cook:20 min

**Ingredients**
- 1 cup of Chopped papaya
- 1/2 cup of Mung dal
- 2 tbsp Chopped onion
- 2 tbsp Chopped garlic
- 2 pcs Green chilies
- one pc Red chili
- 1/2 tsp Turmeric powder
- 2 tbsp Oil
- Salt
- 1/2 tsp Whole cumin

**Directions:**
Cook papaya, mung dal, onion, green chilies, garlic, salt, oil, turmeric powder, and water in a pan. Mash with a masher once the water has dried. Heat oil in a frying pan. Fry the onion, garlic, red chile, and cumin till brown. Now incorporate this into the dal.

Cook for around 2 to 5 minutes. Sprinkle some freshly cut coriander leaves on top and turn off the heat.

# POTATO CURRY RECIPE

Servings:4
Prep:10-15 min Cook:30 min

**Ingredients**
- Two pcs Potatoes
- 1 tsp Chopped onion
- 5-6 pcs Green chilies
- 1/2 tsp Turmeric powder
- Salt
- 2 tbsp Oil

**Directions:**

Potatoes should be cut into tiny pieces. Cook potatoes, green chilies, salt, turmeric powder, and water in a pan.

Once the water has been decreased to half, mash a few potatoes using a potato masher—heat oil in a frying pan. Fry the chopped onion and green chilies till brown. Add this to the potato curry now.

Cook for around 2 to 5 minutes. If desired, sprinkle chopped fresh coriander leaves and turn off the heat. Serve at room temperature with roti, paratha, or luchi.

# DESSERT RECIPES

## MILK AND EGG CARAMEL PUDDING RECIPE

Servings:4
Prep:20-25 min Cook:30 min

**Ingredients**
- 2 pcs Egg
- 3/4 cup of Sugar
- 1 cup of Milk
- 1/2 tsp Vanilla essence

**Directions:**
Caramel is made using 1/4 cup sugar and 1 tbsp water. Caramelize the sugar in the pot that will be used to set the pudding. Allow it to cool before putting it. Beat all the eggs and the rest of the sugar with a fork in a different bowl. Then whisk in the milk.

Additionally, add vanilla essence and combine. You may omit vanilla essence or substitute cardamom powder if you dislike it. Now sift this mixture into the pot in which the caramel was set. Take 2/3 cup of water to a boil in a pan big enough for another pot. Place a stand within the water after it begins to boil, then add the pudding pot. Bake at a lower temperature while covering. Use a toothpick to test the pudding after 30 to 35 minutes. When the toothpick emerges clean, it is finished. If wet, cook for a few more minutes.

Then allow it cool to room temperature fully. Then chill it for 2 hours. After 2 hours, gently de-mold the pudding and serve cold.

# ROSHOGOLLA RECIPE

Servings:5
Prep:35-40 min Cook:50 min

**Ingredients**
- 1 and 1/2 liters Full cream liquid milk
- 1/2 cup of Yogurt
- 1 cup of Sugar
- 1 tsp Milk powder
- 2 tbsp Flour
- Cardamom powder

**Directions:**
Bring milk to a rolling boil. Stir in the beaten yogurt while the mixture is still simmering. Within 30 seconds, you will observe that the milk begins to separate its fat like cheese. This is referred to as chhana. Drain, wash with a cheesecloth, and allow to dry for 30 minutes. Squeeze not to drain water. Allow the water to drain normally.
Knead chhana for 5-8 minutes using one teaspoon of flour, one teaspoon of sugar, one teaspoon of milk powder, and a pinch of cardamom powder. Then divide the mixture into equal little pieces and roll it into a spherical ball.

While kneading chhana in a large saucepan, bring sugar and 3 cups of boiled water. When the sugar has dissolved and the water has come to a boil, add the roshogollas and simmer for 15 mins over medium-high heat without a lid.

Cook for another 10 minutes, adding 1/2 cup boiling water. Then, combine 1 tbsp flour and 2 tbsp water in a bowl. Gradually incorporate this mixture into the syrup and simmer, covered, for 15 minutes on medium-low heat. After 15 minutes, check on roshogolla. To test roshogolla, remove one from the syrup and place it in a water bowl. If roshogolla is immediately submerged in water, it is properly cooked. If not, continue cooking for an additional 5-7 minutes.

Please turn off the heat and leave it alone for at least two hours to cool. Serve at room temperature.

## EASY SUJIR BARFI HALWA RECIPE

Servings:4
Prep:5-7 min Cook:20 min

**Ingredients**
- 1 cup of Semolina
- 1/2 cup of Sugar
- 2 tbsp Ghee
- 1/4 tsp powder Cardamom
- 1/4 tsp powder of cinnamon
- 1 and 1/2 cups of Liquid milk or water
- Salt

**Directions:**
Roast semolina in a pan over medium-low heat. Add one tablespoon of ghee and stir thoroughly when it becomes light brown. Continue roasting for another minute. Then kill the flame and set it away. Bring 1 and 1/2 cups milk or water, sugar, cinnamon, cardamom, and salt to a boil in the same pan. Then gradually add the toasted semolina and simmer for 5 to 7 minutes at a medium temperature. When the semolina is entirely cooked and the water has evaporated, add the remaining ghee and stir thoroughly. Now extinguish the flame. Clarified butter a dish. Distribute the semolina evenly over the platter. Allow it to cool fully. Then cut into desired shapes and serve.

**Note:** If you want, you can add raisins and chopped nuts.

## MASHED GREEN MANGO

**Ingredients**
- 2 pcs Green mango
- 1 tsp Whole Mustard
- 2/3 pcs Green chili
- Salt
- Sugar
- 1/2 pcs Dried red chili
- As needed Black salt

**Directions:**
Peel or grate mango into thin slices and tiny bits. Put aside. Now, prepare mustard and green chile paste. Combine the mango chunks, this paste, salt, and sugar in a large bowl. It is now ready to serve.

## MANGO CHUTNEY

**Ingredients**
- 2 pcs Green mango, big size
- 1/2 cup of Jaggery
- 1/2 cup of Mustard oil
- 1/2 tsp Ginger paste
- 1/2 tsp Garlic paste
- 2 tsp Roasted Five spices mix (Panch foron) powder
- 1 tsp Roasted cumin powder
- 1 tsp Roasted coriander powder
- Salt
- 1 tbsp Vinegar
- 1 tsp Dried red chili powder

**Directions:**
Mangoes should be cut into tiny pieces and washed. Now properly boil and drain them. They may be mashed with a potato masher, fork, or spoon.
In a pan, heat the oil. Add the garlic-ginger paste and whisk for a few seconds. Combine the mashed mango, salt, chili powder, coriander powder, and cumin powder in a bowl. Continue stirring until everything is well combined. Stir in jaggery for a minute. Continue

stirring in the five-spice combination (Panch foron) powder and vinegar.
The mixture should be allowed to cool once the oil has been removed. It may now be preserved in a glass jar for approximately six months without sunlight.

Serve with rice, pulao, khichuri, biriyani, or anything your heart desires.

## GULAB JAMUN RECIPE
Servings:6
Prep:25-30 min Cook:30 min
**Ingredients**
- 1 cup of Milk powder
- 2 tbsp Wheat flour
- 1 tsp Baking powder
- 1 tbsp Ghee
- 3-4 tbsp Liquid milk
- 1 cup of Sugar
- Just a pinch/one pcs Cardamom powder/whole
- 1 cup of Water
- Vegetable-soybean oil
- 2 tbsp Semolina

**Directions:**
Semolina should be soaked in 2 tbsp liquid milk and set aside. Combine milk powder, flour, baking powder, ghee, and soaked semolina in a large mixing basin until thoroughly combined. Then, adding liquid milk at room temperature in stages forms a dough. When the substance feels sticky, it is ready. Maintain for ten minutes. Then, using little balls similar to Gulab Jamun, double the size of the balls. Now, heat oil to very low heat in a different pan. Optionally, 1 tbsp ghee can be added for flavor. Slowly fry Gulab Jamuns for around 10-15 minutes on low heat. They should be removed from the oil when they get a dark brown shade. It should be set aside. Add water and sugar to a big, deep saucepan. Bring the mixture to a boil. Now add the sugar syrup to the fried Gulab Jamuns. Cook for 10 minutes over medium heat, covered. Then extinguish the flame and leave it for two

hours. After two hours, the Gulap Jamuns will have soaked up enough sugar syrup to double in size. It is now ready to serve.

## PLUM CHUTNEY

**Ingredients**
- 500 gm Dried plum
- 1 cup of Sugarcane jaggery
- 1 tbsp Punch foron (Five spices mix)
- 1 tsp Dried red chili powder
- Salt

**Directions:**
Thoroughly wash plums a few times. Boil them in salt water and drain well. In a pan, heat some water and jaggery. When the jaggery has melted, add the boiling plums and continue stirring. Add the chili powder and the five-spice "Panch Foron" powder mixture. Combine everything thoroughly and continue stirring. When the mixture becomes sticky, turn off the heat.

When it cools, it loses its stickiness and dries. Please keep it in a glass jar away from direct sunlight for approximately six months.

## VERMICELLI IN MILK RECIPE

Servings:4
Prep:10-15 min Cook:30 min

**Ingredients**
- 200 gm Vermicelli
- 1 liter Liquid milk
- Dry nuts & raisins
- 2 tbsp Ghee
- 1/2 cup of Sugar
- 1/2 tsp Cinnamon-cardamom powder
- Salt

**Directions:**
Roast dry nuts in a pan over medium-low heat with ghee. Set them aside on low-medium heat and roast vermicelli in the same pan when they turn brown. When it reaches a light brown color, please switch off the heat and put it aside. Meanwhile, in the same pan, bring the

milk to a boil. Bring to a boil with cinnamon, cardamom, and salt. Then, gradually add the toasted vermicelli and simmer for another 5 to 7 minutes at a medium temperature.

When the semolina is 80 percent done, include the sugar and continue cooking for 2-3 mins more. Then, when it is thoroughly done, turn off the heat and sprinkle roasted dry nuts and raisins on top before serving.

## EGG HALWA RECIPE

Servings:4
Prep:10-15 min Cook:20 min

**Ingredients**

- 4 pcs egg
- 1 cup of Liquid milk
- 1/2 cup of Milk powder
- 1/2 cup of Ghee
- 1 cup of Sugar
- Just a pinch of salt
- 1 tbsp Semolina
- 1/2 tsp Cardamom powder

**Directions:**

Grease a mold with ghee beforehand. Put aside.

Combine all items in a blender jug. Blend briskly for 2-4 minutes or until sugar dissolves. Please put them in a pan now. Now adjust the flame to a medium setting. With a spatula or whisk, stir this mixture continuously and patiently. Continue until completely dry. After around 5 to 7 minutes, it becomes thick. Continue to stir. Remove them from the pan when the water evaporates and the ghee starts to come out. Spread evenly in the mold, squeeze, and cut into desired size and shape. Then chill them for 2 hours to set. They are prepared to assist.

# MILK COOKIES RECIPE

Servings:4
Prep:20-25 min Cook:30 min
**Ingredients**
- 1 tbsp Butter
- 2 tbsp Icing sugar
- 1/4 cup of Cornflour
- 2 tbsp Flour
- 1/4 cup of Milk powder
- 1/2 tsp Baking powder
- 2 tsp Liquid milk

**Directions:**
Take a bowl. Take butter and sugar and mix. With a spoon, combine well. Add corn flour, milk powder, flour, and baking powder to a strainer set over a bowl. Mix well. Add the liquid milk and combine everything thoroughly.

Now knead the dough briefly before slicing it into tiny pieces. Make little balls and press them to produce the shape of a biscuit or cookie. Oil or grease a baking tray. Arrange the biscuits on top of it. Preheat oven or baking pan to desired temperature.

Bake at 160°C for 15-17 minutes in the oven or 25-30 minutes on shallow heat in a pan with a stand. Then keep away from them and allow them to cool fully. You may serve or keep the meal for up to 15 days in an airtight box.

# CHANAR JILAPI RECIPE

Servings:6
Prep:30-35 min Cook:30 min

**Ingredients**
- 1 and 1/2 liters Liquid milk
- 5 tsp Flour
- 2 tsp Milk powder
- 2 tsp Semolina
- 1/2 tsp Baking powder
- 1 tsp Ghee
- 1/4 tsp Cardamom powder
- 1 and 1/2 cups of Sugar
- 1 cup of Water
- Oil
- 1/2 cup of Plain yogurt

**Directions:**

Bring milk to a rolling boil. Stir in the beaten yogurt while the mixture is still simmering. Within 30 seconds, you will observe that the milk begins to separate its fat the same way as cheese does. This is referred to as chhana. Pour into a cheesecloth-lined strainer set over a basin so it can drain. Channa should be washed with cold tap water and drained. Allow an hour. Squeeze not to drain water. Allow it to air dry naturally.

Knead chhana for 5-8 minutes using flour, milk powder, semolina, baking powder, ghee, and cardamom powder. Then split into equal little pieces and form chhanar jilapi forms.

Fry jilapis in oil over low heat till brown. It may take between seven and ten minutes. Then remove them and set them away.

Bring sugar, water, and cardamom powder to a boil in a big pan. Then add the fried jilapis and cook for 2 minutes over medium heat.

Now switch off the heat and let them cool fully for at least two hours to be well-saturated. Serve warm to enhance the flavor.

# MALAI CAKE RECIPE

Servings;4
Prep:30-35 min Cook:40 min

## Ingredients

- 1 cup of Wheat flour
- three pcs Eggs
- 1/2 cup of for cake, 1/4 cup of for malai Sugar
- 1/3 cup of Oil
- 1 tsp Baking powder
- 2 tbsp Powder milk
- 3 cups of Liquid milk
- 1/4 tsp Cardamom powder
- Chopped dried nuts & fruits

## Directions:

Combine all dry ingredients, mix, and filter through a strainer. Put aside. In a large bowl, combine eggs at room temperature. If they were in the refrigerator, keep them away at least one hour ago. Separate the egg yolks carefully and set them aside. Now, using a hand beater or whisk, whip the egg whites. Add the icing sugar/sugar gradually and beat thoroughly when it starts to foam. After that, whisk in egg yolks and oil or melted butter in a slow, steady stream.

Now add the combination of the dry ingredient. Add them gradually and stir with a spatula or spoon. Avoid over-mixing or using a hand beater during this step.

Grease a cake mold with oil or butter and line the bottom with parchment or regular paper. Fill it halfway with cake mix/batter. Tap several times to dislodge bubbles. Heat oven to 400 degrees Fahrenheit for 10 mins. Afterward, bake your cake for 20 minutes at 160 degrees Fahrenheit. Use a toothpick to verify after 20 minutes. It's done when a toothpick put in the center of the cake comes out clean. It should take another five minutes in the oven to do the job.

Bring 3 cups of liquid milk, sugar, and cardamom powder to a boil. Reduce 3 cups of milk to two cups. Allow it to cool somewhat. Then pour it over the cake's top. Alternatively, you may sprinkle some dried fruits and nuts on top. Refrigerate it. Allow it to cool fully. After that, serve.

## FALOODA RECIPE

Servings:4
Prep:15-20 min Cook:40 min

### Ingredients

- 1/2 cup of Sago
- 2 cups of Milk
- 1 and 1/2 cup of Sugar
- 2 tsp Agar agar powder
- 2 tsp Milk powder
- Food colors

### Directions:

*To make sago:*

1. Fill a big pan halfway with water and set it aside to warm.
2. Add sago to the water for 10-15 minutes and stir periodically.
3. When the sago has been adequately cooked and has become translucent, turn off the heat.
4. Drain the water and rinse the boiling sago under cold running water.
5. Immerse them in ice-cold water and set them.
6. Watch the video below from Mohabbat Ka Sharbat to learn how to make sago.

To prepare milk malai, boil and combine milk and 2 tbsp sugar in a separate pan. Mix two teaspoons of agar agar powder and 2 tbsp fresh water in a bowl to prepare jello. It should be set aside. Add 2 cups of water and 2/3 cup sugar to a separate pan and bring it to a boil. Pour in the agar-agar and whisk rapidly. Then pour it into a box or any other container. Add your preferred food coloring and lay aside for two hours to set. To prepare sugar syrup, combine 1/4 cup sugar and 1/4 cup fresh water in a separate pan and boil. Now place everything in the refrigerator to chill. Check out the Mohabbat Ka Sharbat recipe video to learn how to make Sugar Syrup.

Add ice to a mug or tumbler, followed by the cooked sago, malai, sugar syrup, and jello. Garnish with Rooh-Afza and, if desired, sprinkle dried fruits and nuts over faluda before serving.

## INSTANT SHAHI TUKRA RECIPE

Servings:4
Prep:10-15 min Cook:20 min
**Ingredients**
- 6 pcs Bread
- 2 cups of Liquid milk
- 2 tbsp Powder milk
- 1 tsp Custard powder
- 1/4 cup of Sugar
- 1/4 tsp Cardamom powder
- 1/2 cup of Ghee
- Mixed dry nuts

**Directions:**
Fry nuts briefly in ghee and set aside. Now, heat the ghee over medium-low heat and cook the bread slices till golden brown. Maintain on a serving tray. Combine liquid milk, milk powder, custard powder, sugar, and cardamom powder in a pan. Set the heat to high and continue stirring until the mixture thickens into malai. Now pour the malai over the bread and allow it to cool and soak. Then refrigerate and serve cool. While serving, sprinkle dry nuts over the top.

## SPICY KASHMIRI ACHAR RECIPE

Servings:4
Prep:10-15 min Cook:25 min

**Ingredients**
- two pcs (medium in size) Green mango
- 1 cup of Sugar
- 1/2 cup of Vinegar
- 1 tbsp Ginger slices
- 1/2 tbsp Chopped dried red chilies

- 2 pcs Cinnamon
- 2 pcs Cardamom
- 3 pcs Cloves
- Salt
- one pc Bay leaf

**Directions:**
Rinse and drain the mango. Remove the peel and cut it into desired pieces or slices. It should be set aside. Now, boil the sugar, vinegar, and salt in a pan. Add mangoes and boil over low heat until partially. Add the ginger slice, red chilies, and other spices. Cook until the mangoes become translucent. Then extinguish the flame. Please wait for it to cool down early before putting it in the refrigerator for 2 to 4 months.

# SWEET YOGURT RECIPE

Servings:4
Prep:10 min Cook:20 min
**Ingredients**
- 3 cups of Milk
- 1/2 cup of Sugar
- 1/2 cup of sour yogurt

**Directions:**
Combine sugar and water in a pan. Bring to a boil over low-medium heat. When it begins to change into caramel, add the milk. Continue stirring until the mixture is about two-thirds full. Please bring it to a cool to lukewarm temperature, but not cold. Using a fork, beat the sour yogurt to a smooth paste and combine it with the milk. Before using, drain excess water from the curd.

Pour the milk mixture from a slight height into a dry bowl or pot to create foam. Remember that the bowl or pot to set the yogurt must be entirely dry. With a towel, cover it and leave it for at least 8 hours or overnight.

Store the yogurt for another 5-6 hours if it has not been set. After that, you may serve.

## SAGO KESARI RECIPE

Servings:3
Prep:10 min Cook:30 m

**Ingredients**
- 200 gm sago
- 1/3 cup of Sugar
- 2 tbsp Ghee
- 6/7 pcs Cashew nuts
- 2 pcs Cinnamon
- 2 pcs Cardamom
- Food color

**Directions:**

The sago should be washed and soaked overnight. Then drain thoroughly.

Now, in a pan, heat the ghee. Shallow fried the cashew nuts and set aside when done. Combine cinnamon, cardamom, and soaked sago in a small bowl. Fry for around 1 to 2 minutes. Mix sugar and food coloring well.

Add the needed water and simmer over low heat until the sago is thoroughly cooked. Add additional ghee and cooked cashew nuts and stir well. Serve immediately after extinguishing the flame.

# POWDER ROSHMALAI

Servings:4
Prep:15-20 min Cook:15 min

## Ingredients
- 1 and 1/2 cups of Milk powder
- 3 cups of Liquid milk
- 1/4 tsp Cardamom powder
- 1/2 cup of Sugar
- 1/2 tsp Baking powder
- 1tbsp Ghee
- 1 pcs Egg

## Directions:
Ghee, milk powder, and baking powder are mixed in a big mixing bowl. Then, adding a well-beaten egg at room temperature in stages form a sticky dough. When the substance feels sticky, it is ready. Take a 5-minute break. Then form little balls, bearing in mind that they will eventually double in size.

Add 2 and 1/2 cups liquid milk and sugar to a big deep saucepan. Bring the mixture to a boil. Avoid overcooking them. Now pour the milk over the balls. Cover and cook for 4-6 mins on low to medium heat. Occasionally, shake them with the handle.

Combine the rest of the milk powder and warm water in a different bowl. Then remove the top and pour in the milk. Shake gently to combine. Cover and cook for another 5 minutes. After 5 minutes, extinguish the flame and leave it off for 2 hours. Rasmalai is ready to serve after 2 hours.

# EXCEPTIONAL RECIPE

## EGG BIRYANI RECIPE

Servings:5
Prep:20 min Cook:1 hr

### Ingredients

- 5 pcs Boiled eggs
- 6 pcs Large potato pieces
- 1 cup of Chopped onion
- 1 tbsp Ginger-garlic paste
- 1/2 packet biriyani masala
- 2 tsp Sugar
- 4 pcs Green chilies
- 10/12 pcs Raisins
- 2 tsp Ghee
- 1/2 cup of Oil
- 2 cups or 500 gm Chinigura/aromatic rice
- Salt

### Directions:

Rice should be appropriately washed and dried. With a fork or toothpick, poke potatoes and eggs all over. Combine them with a sprinkle of turmeric powder and cook them in a low amount of oil. It should be set aside.

Now, in a pan, heat the oil. Fry the chopped onion till golden brown. Save some of the fried onion for later use. Then, along with the remaining onion, add the ginger-garlic paste. Fry for a few minutes. Combine ready-made biryani masala, salt, and beaten yogurt in a small bowl. Cook for approximately 2-3 minutes. A low quantity of water can be added to prevent the spices from burning.

Add fried potatoes, eggs, and a bit of water. Cook for 5-7 minutes, stirring periodically, or until the potatoes are cooked. After that, remove the eggs and potatoes and save the masala for the following step.

Now stir in the pre-washed and drained rice and sauté for 2-3 minutes: three cups boiling water and 1 cup warm liquid milk. You may substitute powdered milk for liquid milk. Cook for 5 minutes on medium-high heat with the lid closed.

Mix well with the eggs, potatoes, sugar, green chiles, and raisins. Cover with a cover and cook for 10-15 minutes on medium-low heat. Cover with the lid and apply ghee and fried onion over the top. Switch off the flame and let it on the burner for another 10-15 minutes. After that, your biryani is ready to serve.

## ILISH PULAO RECIPE

Servings:5
Prep:20-25 min Cook:45 min

**Ingredients**
- 5 pcs Hilsa fish
- 2 cups of Normal rice
- 1 cup of Chopped onion
- 10-12 pcs Green chilies
- 1/2 cup of Oil
- 1 and 1/2 tsp Turmeric powder
- 2 cups of Coconut milk
- Salt

**Directions:**

Hilsa fish should be cut into pieces. Properly clean and drain. The tissue paper may collect excess water—Marinate fish fillets in a small amount of salt and turmeric powder.

Now, in a pan, heat the oil. Fry both sides of the salmon until golden brown. They should be set aside. Fry 3/4 cup onion and 7/8 cup green chilies till golden brown. Set this away as well. In the oil, include the remaining onion and chiles. Thirty seconds in a hot pan. 2 cups coconut milk, 3 cup water, salt, and turmeric powder. However, if desired, you may add sugar in a very tiny amount, such as 2 tsp. Carry to a boil, covered with a lid. Then add rice that has been rinsed and drained previously. Cover and simmer over medium-high warmth until the chicken is 80 percent done and the liquid evaporates.

Incorporate fried fish pieces, onion, and chilies into the rice and conceal them. Cover with a cover and cook on low heat for 10 to 15 minutes. After 15 minutes, extinguish the flame and cover it for 10 minutes. Carefully remove the fish chunks from the rice by lifting it up and down. Serve hilsa pilaf rice with salad at room temperature.

## BANANA CAKE RECIPE

**Ingredients**
- Two pcs Well ripened banana
- 1 cup of Wheat flour
- 2 pcs Egg
- 1/2 cup of Sugar
- 1/2 cup of oil/butter
- 1 tsp Baking powder
- 1/2 tsp Baking soda
- 1/2 cup of liquid milk
- 1 tsp Vanilla essence

**Directions:**

First, mix all dry components in a bowl and mix and filter through a sieve. Put aside. Bananas should be peeled and mashed finely using a fork/spoon. This should be set aside.

Take two room-temperature eggs and place them in a big dish. If they are refrigerated, keep them away from the refrigerator for at least one hour. Now, using a hand beater or hand whisk, beat eggs. Add the icing sugar/sugar gradually and beat thoroughly when it is frothy. After that, add oil or butter progressively and beat again. Then add the mashed bananas and beat thoroughly to combine.

It's time to include the combination of the dry ingredient. Add them gradually and stir with a spatula or spoon. Avoid over-mixing and beat with a hand beater throughout this step. Once the batter is smooth, whisk in the milk and vanilla extract with a spatula.

Oil or butter a cake mold. Fill it halfway with cake mix/batter. Tap several times to remove bubbles.

For 10 min, heat the oven to 400 degrees Fahrenheit. Then bake your cake for 45 minutes at 160°C. After 40 minutes, use a toothpick to check. The cake is ready to serve if a toothpick in the center comes out clean. If not, bake for a further 5-6 minutes.

# PALM CAKE

Servings:4
Prep:20 min Cook:30 min

**Ingredients**
- 1 cup of Palm pulp
- 2 cups of Rice flour
- 1/2 cup of All-purpose flour
- 3/4 cup of Sugar
- Salt
- fry Oil

**Directions:**

Combine palm pulp, rice flour, all-purpose flour, sugar, salt, and milk in a mixing bowl. Gradually add water until a smooth batter is formed. For 2-3 minutes, whisk the batter until smooth. For 30 minutes, cover and rest.
After 30 minutes, stir the batter with your hands or for 5 minutes with a whisk. Preheat a frying pan with oil for deep frying. To begin, heat oil over a medium burner. Then reduce to low heat and add a tablespoon of batter to the oil. Allow it to rise and puff up after that. You may tap oil on the top with a spoon or spatula to cause it to rise. Then fry both sides until golden and cooked thoroughly. Drain the oil through a sieve and place it on tissue paper to absorb any leftover oil. After that, serve.

# INSTANT MANGO PICKLE RECIPE

Servings:6
Prep:20-25 min Cook:30 min

**Ingredients**
- 1 kg Green mango
- 1 tsp of every Ginger-garlic paste
- 250 gm Mustard oil
- 2 pcs Dried red chili
- 2 pcs Bay leaves
- 1/4 tsp Whole mustard
- 2 tbsp Sugar
- 2 tsp Vinegar
- Salt
- 1 tsp Turmeric powder

**Directions:**
Wash and drain the mango. Then peel and slice. Take them and put them in a basin. Combine salt and turmeric powder well with your hand. It should be set aside.

Now, in a frying pan, combine one teaspoon panch foron (unique five-spice blend), four dried red chilies, 1/2 teaspoon cumin, 1/2 teaspoon coriander, and 1/2 teaspoon mustard and roast over medium heat until brown. Then remove them, grind them, and set them aside.

In a saucepan, heat the oil. Combine the red chili, bay leaves, and whole mustard seeds. Fry for a few minutes. When they begin to bubble, add the mangoes and stir well to combine. Cook for around 2-5 minutes. This time, incorporate ginger-garlic pastes. Cook for an additional 5 minutes. Mix half the ground spice powder, sugar, and salt in a bowl. Combine and cook over a low heat setting.

When the mangoes are cooked thoroughly, add the vinegar. For another 5 minutes, mix everything and cook on the stove. Remove the food from the stove and let it cool down. Then, spread the rest of the spice mix over the top and mix it well. When it begins to leak oil, switch off the flame. Allow it to cool completely before using. After that, please keep it in a clean, dry glass jar. It will keep for one month or two months at room temperature. You may also retain this in the refrigerator for approximately six months. Consume this pickle alongside your favorite foods.

## JACKFRUIT WITH PRAWN RECIPE

Servings: 6
Prep: 30-35 min Cook: 45 min

**Ingredients**
- 500 gm Raw Jackfruit
- 200 gm Prawn/shrimp
- 1/3 cup of Chopped onion
- 1 tsp of every Ginger-garlic paste
- 1 tsp Cumin powder
- 1 tsp Red chili powder
- 1 tsp Turmeric powder
- 2 Pcs Cinnamon
- 3 Pcs Cardamom
- one pc Bay leaf
- 3 Pcs Cloves
- 1/2 tsp Roasted garam masala powder
- 1/3 cup of Vegetable oil
- Salt
- 1 tsp Sugar

**Directions:**

Remove the prickly jackfruit peel using a large sharp knife and chop the interior white soft jackfruit cells into small pieces, including the soft seeds. Grease your hands with oil before chopping jackfruit to avoid sticking. Bring some water and bring it to a boil. Let it boil for about two or three minutes. Then thoroughly wash and drain. With salt, turmeric powder, and oil, fry the prawns/shrimp in a skillet on the stove. It should be set aside.

Now, in a pan, heat the oil. Fry the cinnamon, cardamom, cloves, onion, and bay leaf for a few minutes. Cook until the raw scent of the ginger-garlic paste, cumin powder, red chili powder, turmeric powder, and salt has disappeared. Now whisk in the jackfruit to combine with the spices. Cook, covered, for 15-20 minutes with 1 and 1/2 cups water.

When the water has evaporated completely, add the fried prawns/shrimps and simmer for 2-3 minutes. Cook for another 5-10 minutes, adding 1 cup of water and sugar. When the jackfruit is appropriately cooked, mash a little of it. Remove the remove from heat and stir in the roasted garam masala powder (cinnamon, cardamom, clove, and black pepper). Serve at room temperature with rice, roti, or paratha.

## DRUMSTICK CURRY RECIPE

Servings:6
Prep:10 min Cook:25 min
**Ingredients**
- 250 gm Drumstick
- one pc Medium size Potato
- 2 tbsp Chopped onion
- 1 tsp Dried red chili powder
- 1 tsp Mustard paste
- 1/2 tsp Cumin powder
- 1 tsp Turmeric powder
- 2 pcs Tomato
- 2 tbsp Vegetable oil
- Salt

**Directions:**
In a pan, heat the oil. Add the onion and stir occasionally. Stir in drumsticks, potatoes, salt, and chili powder. Now include 1 cup of water and cook until the water evaporates. Include the turmeric powder and stir for a few minutes when the water evaporates. Add the mustard paste and cumin powder and whisk for a few minutes to thoroughly combine everything. Make your curry the right consistency by adding 1+1/2 cups of fresh water or as much as you need. Then cover and continue to cook until everything is properly cooked.

Cook the meat without adding the tomato pieces for a few more minutes. Drumstick curry is an easy, healthful, and delectable dish best served warmly with plain rice.

# BANANA CHIPS RECIPE

Servings:2
Prep:15-20 min Cook:15 min

**Ingredients**
- 4 pcs Green Banana
- Vegetable soybean oil
- 1/2 tsp Black salt
- 1/4 tsp Red chili powder

**Directions:**
Peel bananas and immerse them in water to prevent black spots. Then, wipe away any remaining moisture using kitchen tissue or a clean towel.
Slice or grate bananas into thin pieces using a slicer or grater. Fry soon after slicing to prevent them from becoming black. Now, in a pan, heat some oil. Patience is needed when frying those banana slices for 2-3 minutes at a medium temperature. When they become brown and seem crispy, keep them away from the oil and put them on tissue paper to absorb any remaining oil.
Toss thoroughly with black salt and red chili powder. You are now ready to serve your banana chips. Serve alongside your preferred sauce or ketchup.

# RICE FLOUR VAPE/BHAPA PITHA RECIPE

Servings:4
Prep:40 min Cook:1 hr

**Ingredients**
- 2 cups of Rice flour
- 1 cup of grated coconut
- 1 cup of Jaggery
- Salt
- vapa-pitha-recipe

**Directions:**
Rice flour and salt should be combined in a big bowl. Combine well and add regular water gradually. Once, add a small amount of water and stir with your hand. Do not include the entire amount of water at once. We only need to moisten the flour. Add water gradually and massage with your hands. The flour combination would be neither

dough nor batter but relatively moist. When finished, set aside for 5 minutes.

Now sift the flour through a screen to separate the refined grains from the balled grains. This phase is necessary to perfect your pithas. Now break the balls by hand and massage and squeeze them again to refine them.

Fill a big saucepan or deep pan half with water. Arrange a pitha mold on top of it. If there is no mold, lay an aluminum foil paper over the entrance of the pan to prevent vapor from leaving. Then, poke holes around a 5- to 6-inch-wide circle in the middle with a fork or toothpick. Increase to medium-high heat and boil a large pot of water. To begin, pour some flour mixture into a small bowl or Katori. Then put coconut on top, followed by jaggery. Now add another layer of the flour mixture. Please do not attempt to press it. Fill the dish to the same level. Cover with a damp net cloth or any other type of cheesecloth.

Place it on the aluminum foil, tap it with your fingers to dislodge the pitha from the bowl, wrap the net fabric around it, and cover it with a lid or something else that will prevent the vapor from escaping. Wait 5–7 minutes. Then inspect it and, if necessary, remove it. Using a spatula or big spoon, carefully unwrap the pitha from the cloth and put it on a platter. Create other pithas in the same manner. Serve heated to get the most out of it.

## CHITOI PITHA RECIPE WITHOUT RICE FLOUR

**Ingredients**
- 1 cup of Chinigura/kalijeera rice
- 1/2 cup of Normal rice
- 2 tbsp Scraped coconut
- 1 & 1/2 cups of lukewarm water
- 1 tsp Vegetable oil
- 1 tsp Water
- Salt

**Directions:**
Both rice should be well washed and soaked for at least 8 hours or overnight. Drain any excess liquid.

Add 1+half cups lukewarm water and salt to the rice and whisk until smooth. Avoid using incredibly hot or boiling water. Always begin with lukewarm water. Place a strainer on a bowl and pour the rice batter to remove any remaining particles. Now, beat 2-3 minutes using a spoon or hand whisk. For 15 minutes, cover and rest. After 15 minutes, optionally add scraped coconut.

You may use metallic, earthenware, or nonstick pan specially designed for Chitoi Pitha. Mix 1 tsp water and 1 tsp oil in a bowl, and use a fresh cloth or tissue paper to lubricate the pan or mold before pouring the pitha batter. Preheat the pan over medium heat, oil the mold, and add enough batter. Cook covered. Assure that no air escapes via the lid.

Ensure the food is cooked for about 4 to 5 mins on low heat or until it's crunchy enough. The more holes in the pitha, the more flawless it is. If the pitha has no or very few holes or seems solid, thin the batter with a few drops of lukewarm water. Rep the procedure to create all pithas. Remember that the first 1-2 pithas are only sometimes beneficial. Continue creating with patience; the pithas that follow must be flawless. Serve these pithas warm with your preferred sauce, jaggery, coconut scraped, pickle, or meat curry.

## CHOTPOTI RECIPE WITH SPECIAL SPICES MIX

Servings:6
Prep:10-15 min Cook:30 min
**Ingredients**
- 250 gm Gram
- 1 tbsp Chopped onion
- 1/2 tsp Garlic paste
- 1/2 tsp Ginger paste
- 1/2 tsp Turmeric powder
- 1/2 tsp Cumin powder
- 2 tbsp Vegetable oil
- 1/2 tsp Cinnamon powder
- Salt
- 1/2 tsp Cardamom powder
- Water

- one pc Potato
- 6-7 pcs Sliced green chilies

*Serving ingredients*
- Chopped onion
- Chopped green chilies
- Chopped cucumber
- Chopped tomato
- Chopped coriander leaves
- Grated boiled egg
- Black salt
- Lemon juice
- Crackers
- Tamarind

**Directions:**

Grams should be cleaned and submerged in water for at least four hours. If you have time, soak it overnight. Then repeat the process and thoroughly drain.

In a pressure cooker, heat 2 tbsp vegetable/soybean oil. Alternatively, you may use a pan. However, a pressure cooker cooks food more quickly. Then add the onion and sliced chilies and continue stirring for a few minutes. Now add the ginger and garlic pastes, as well as the salt. Include a tiny bit of water to prevent the spices from burning afterward. Stir in cumin powder, turmeric powder (if using), cinnamon, and cardamom powders till brown.

Now combine the grams with a complete medium-sized peeled potato (optional) and whisk for 2-3 minutes to thoroughly combine them with the spices. Water should be added. Your desired consistency determines the amount of water required. On medium heat, cover and simmer until 6-8 whistles. The gram should be cooked for a moderate amount of time. While the grams are frying, let's prepare that secret unique chotpoti spice blend! Roast and grind to a fine powder 4 dried red chilies, 1 teaspoon Panch foron (unique five-spice blend), 4 cloves, 1/2 teaspoon black pepper, 1 cinnamon stick, 3 cardamom sticks, 1 teaspoon mustard, 1 teaspoon cumin, and 3 teaspoon coriander. We will only utilize a tiny amount; the remainder may be stored in an airtight jar for 3-4 months without sunshine.

Now it's time to serve; the ingredients will vary according to your preference and flavor. Combine the cooked grains and potato in a bowl, partly mashing the potato with a fork. Combine thoroughly with tamarind water (tamarind was steeped in water for 30 minutes, pressed to extract the puree, and drained). 1 tsp pre-made unique spice blend Add cucumber, tomato, coriander leaves, green chile, onion, crackers (nimki/fuchka), shredded cooked eggs (optional), another 1/2 teaspoon special spices mix, and black salt to taste.

## GREEN BANANA CUTLET

**Ingredients**
- 4 pcs Green banana
- 1/2 tsp of every Ginger-garlic paste
- 2 tbsp Fried onion
- 1 tsp Chopped green chilies
- 1/2 tsp Roasted coriander powder
- 1/2 tsp Cumin powder
- Cardamom powder
- Chopped coriander leaves
- Salt
- 2 tbsp Cornflour
- Vegetable oil

**Directions:**
Cut four green bananas in halves. Now bring them to a boil and drain. Then peel out and mash the bananas in a bowl.
Combine fried onion, green chilies, coriander leaves, ginger-garlic pastes, cumin powder, roasted coriander powder, cardamom powder, salt, and cornflour in a small bowl. Combine everything well.
Using a tiny quantity of banana mash, form it into a cutlet or patty and coat it with breadcrumbs. Repeat the procedure to create all of the cutlets. Then refrigerate the cutlets for 30 minutes.
In a frying pan, heat the oil. On medium-low heat, shallow-fried the cutlets until they are a deep brown. Then remove them from the oil and set them on a tissue to absorb any excess oil. Serve with your choice of rice or ketchup.

# ELEPHANT ARUM STEM RECIPE

Servings:4
Prep:15 min Cook:20 min
**Ingredients**
- 5-6 pcs Elephant arum stem
- 250 gm Jack fruit seeds
- 6-7 pcs Sliced green chilies
- 2 tbsp Chopped onion
- 2 pcs Cinnamon
- 2 pcs Cardamom
- 1 tsp Mustard paste
- 1/2 tsp Cumin powder
- 1/2 tsp of every Ginger-garlic paste
- 1 tsp Turmeric powder
- 1/4 cup of Vegetable Oil
- Salt
- one pc Bay leaf

**Directions:**
Thinly slice elephant arum stems and jackfruit seeds. Thoroughly clean and drain. Two cups of water should come to a boil. Then, cook the food for about two to three minutes. Then drain and thoroughly rinse with regular water.

Now, in a saucepan, heat some vegetable oil. Stir in the chopped onions, chiles, bay leaf, cinnamon, and cardamom for 2 minutes to eliminate any raw aromas. This time, incorporate arum chunks and seeds. Provide a pleasing mixture. Season with salt, chilies, and a splash of water, cover the pan and simmer for 5-7 minutes or until the chilies are soft. Add mustard paste, cumin powder, garlic, ginger, and turmeric powder, and continue cooking until the mustard paste releases oil. Add some water and continue cooking for an additional 5 to 10 minutes. Once the water has fully evaporated, turn off the heat and serve warm.

# BRINJAL/EGGPLANT/AUBERGINE PASTE

**Ingredients**
- one pc Brinjal/eggplant
- one pc Potato
- 5-6 pcs Dal Bori
- 2 tbsp Chopped onion
- 1tsp Chopped garlic
- 2-3 pcs Dried red chili
- 3-4 pcs Green chili
- 1/2 tsp Turmeric powder
- 1 tsp Cumin
- 2 tbsp Vegetable oil
- two piece Bay leaves
- Salt

**Directions:**
Potatoes, brinjal/eggplant/aubergine, and aubergine should all be cut into small pieces. Thoroughly clean and drain. Now, boil the potatoes, brinjal/eggplant/aubergine, and add salt, turmeric powder, and green chilies in low water until the water evaporates.

Now, in a saucepan, heat some oil. Combine the onion, garlic, dried red chilies, bay leaves, and cumin in a small bowl. Stir constantly until the mixture becomes a golden brown hue.

Now whisk in smashed berries for 1 to 2 minutes. Then add the boiled brinjal/eggplant/aubergine paste, mix well, and serve warm with plain rice. You may add a few little shrimp for added flavor and texture.

# MASHED CILANTRO/CORIANDER LEAVES

**Ingredients**
- 250 gm Cilantro/coriander leaves
- 2 tbsp Chopped onion
- 6-7 pcs Green chili
- 1tsp Ginger paste
- 1 tsp Garlic paste
- 1 tsp Cumin powder
- 1 tsp Turmeric powder

- 1/2 tsp Cinnamon powder
- 1/2 tsp Cardamom powder
- 2 tbsp Vegetable oil
- Salt
- 1/3 cup of Shrimp

**Directions:**
Mix cilantro/coriander leaves, green chilies, onion, and shrimp in a blender. In a pan, heat the oil. Add the combined mixture and stir for a few minutes. Add the other ingredients and constantly stir until the mixture hardens and releases oil. It's now ready to serve alongside simple rice. Squeeze little lemon juice over each serving for enhanced flavor and taste.

## RICE PUDDING WITH JAGGERY

Servings:6
Prep:10-15 min Cook:20 min
**Ingredients**
- 1/3 cup of Aromatic rice (Kalojeera/Chinigura)
- 1 liter of milk
- 1/2 cup of New Jaggery
- 2 pcs Cinnamon
- 2 pcs Cardamom
- 4-5 pcs Raisin

**Directions:**
Rice should be washed and soaked for two hours. In a saucepan, heat milk. Add the rice and continue cooking on low heat when the milk begins to boil. Stir often to prevent burning.

Everything should be added when the rice is almost done. Then, stir everything together. For a few extra minutes, or until the sauce is thick, keep cooking until the sauce is done. Serve at room temperature.

# NAAN

Prep: 1 hour Cook: 1 hour Servings: 4

**Ingredients**
- 1 1/2 pkg active dry yeast
- 1 tsp sugar
- 4 1/4 cups of all-purpose flour
- 1 1/2 tsp salt
- 1/2 cup of yogurt
- one lightly beaten egg
- 5 tbsp melted ghee

**Steps**

Combine yeast, sugar, and 5 tbsp water in a small bowl. Stir. Allow approximately 5 minutes as far as foamy. Sift flour and salt into a sizeable bowl. In the center, create a well. Combine the egg and yogurt with the yeast mixture. Five tablespoons warm water Stir and pour into the flour thoroughly. Stir from the center outward until the batter is smooth. Incorporate ghee.

Knead on board for 15-20 minutes or in a food processor for roughly 2 minutes. The dough should be malleable but not tacky—place it in a covered basin and set it to double in size (about one hour).

Divide the ball into eight equal halves. Gently knead each ball, flatten it, and shape it into an oval resembling a pear. Place on a baking sheet(s), cover with a moist towel and let around 15 minutes for the dough to rise. Using ghee, brush the surface and sprinkle with seeds. (Optional).

Bake for 9 mins, or until golden brown, in a preheated 450-degree F oven.

# CONCLUSION

Bangladeshi cookbook is a rich compilation of recipes and culinary traditions from Bangladesh, a South Asian country known for its vibrant and flavorful cuisine. This cookbook offers a glimpse into the diverse range of dishes that make up Bangladeshi cuisine, showcasing a combination of influences from Bengali, Mughlai, and other regional culinary traditions.

The cookbook takes readers on a culinary journey, highlighting the unique spices, ingredients, and cooking techniques characteristic of Bangladeshi cuisine. It offers various recipes, ranging from traditional staples like biryani, bhuna, and korma to street food favorites such as pani puri, jhal muri, and samosas.

One of the notable aspects of the Bangladeshi cookbook is its emphasis on fresh and locally sourced ingredients. Many recipes in the book encourage seasonal produce and showcase the importance of using authentic Bangladeshi spices to increase the flavors of the dishes.
Furthermore, the cookbook provides detailed instructions and step-by-step guides, making it accessible for experienced and novice cooks. It shares recipes and provides cultural context and insights into the significance of certain dishes within Bangladeshi culture and traditions.
A Bangladeshi cookbook is a valuable resource for anyone interested in exploring the flavors of Bangladesh and delving into its rich culinary heritage. It celebrates the diversity and vibrancy of Bangladeshi cuisine, offering a delightful array of recipes that individuals from various cultural backgrounds can enjoy.
Moreover, the Bangladeshi cookbook serves as a bridge between different cultures and promotes cultural exchange through food. It provides an opportunity for people from outside Bangladesh to learn about and appreciate the country's unique flavors and cooking techniques. By following the recipes and trying out the dishes, readers

can experience a taste of Bangladesh and develop a deeper understanding of its culinary traditions.

The cookbook also acknowledges the importance of food in fostering social connections and bringing people together. Many of the recipes name included in the book are meant to be shared and enjoyed with family and friends during festive occasions, gatherings, or everyday meals. This aspect reflects the hospitality and warmth deeply ingrained in Bangladeshi culture.

Additionally, the Bangladeshi cookbook highlights the versatility of Bangladeshi cuisine, catering to different dietary preferences and restrictions. It includes a range of vegetarian, vegan, and gluten-free options, ensuring that there is something for everyone to enjoy. This inclusivity demonstrates the adaptability and innovation of Bangladeshi cooking.

In conclusion, the Bangladeshi cookbook not only provides a collection of delicious and authentic recipes but also serves as a cultural ambassador, promoting the rich culinary heritage of Bangladesh to a broader audience. It celebrates the country's diverse flavors, spices, and cooking traditions while fostering a sense of community and gratitude for the power of food to bring people together. Whether you are a perfectly skilled cook or a culinary enthusiast, the Bangladeshi cookbook is an excellent resource for exploring the vibrant and mouth-watering world of Bangladeshi cuisine.

**THE END**

Printed in the USA
CPSIA information can be obtained
at www.ICGtesting.com
LVHW010016170324
774678LV00011B/1183